# Growing in Christian Morality

## Casebook Leader's Guide

Genuine recycled paper with 10% post-consumer waste.
Printed with soy-based ink.

The publishing team included Stephan Nagel, development editor; Brooke E. Saron, copy editor; Barbara Bartelson, production editor and typesetter; Laurie Geisler, cover designer; Cindi Ramm, design director; manufactured by the production services department of Saint Mary's Press.

The acknowledgments continue on page 210.

Printed in the United States of America

Printing: 9 8 7 6 5 4 3 2 1

Year: 2010 09 08 07 06 05 04 03 02

ISBN 0-88489-712-5

Library of Congress Cataloging-in-Publication Data

Crawford Hodapp, Kathleen.
      Growing in Christian morality. Casebook leader's guide / Kathleen Crawford Hodapp.
      p. cm.
ISBN 0-88489-712-5
      1. Christian ethics—Catholic authors. 2. Catholic youth—Religious life. 3. Christian ethics—Study and teaching. 4. Christian education of teenagers. 5. Moral education.
I. Ahlers, Julia. Growing in Christian morality. II. Title.
BJ1249 .C73 2001
241'.042'0712—dc21
                                                                                          2001001027

# Growing in Christian Morality
## Casebook Leader's Guide

by Kathleen Crawford Hodapp

**Saint Mary's Press**
**Christian Brothers Publications**
**Winona, Minnesota**

# Table of Contents

As God's chosen ones, holy and beloved, clothe yourselves with compassion, kindness, humility, meekness, and patience. Bear with one another and, if anyone has a complaint against another, forgive each other; just as the Lord has forgiven you, so you also must forgive. Above all, clothe yourselves with love, which binds everything together in perfect harmony. And let the peace of Christ rule in your hearts, to which indeed you were called in the one body. And be thankful. Let the word of Christ dwell in you richly; teach and admonish one another in all wisdom; and with gratitude in your hearts sing psalms, hymns, and spiritual songs to God. And whatever you do, in word or deed, do everything in the name of the Lord Jesus, giving thanks to God the Father through him.

—Colossians 3:12–17

**Kathleen Crawford Hodapp** is a development editor of Web and curriculum materials at Saint Mary's Press. She taught theology for eleven years at Mercy Academy in Louisville, Kentucky, where she served as department chair. Kat lives in Louisville with her three children, Ellie, Anna, and Joseph, who are constant reminders of God's grace.

# INTRODUCTION

- What does religion have to do with my life?
- How do I know right from wrong?
- How do I make good decisions?

Great questions from teenagers! And what answers do we give them? Learning what Christian morality entails is a very important part of a Catholic teenager's religious education, whether it is part of a high school curriculum, a parish religious education program, or a youth ministry program.

## The Virtuous Life

Catholic education calls young people to a life of virtue. Jesus is the role model for this life; he lived out the moral virtues, which are the building blocks of character.

Character development and moral decision making are related. Moral behaviors are shaped more by the character we have developed than by the rules or principles we learn. In a morality course, it is important to encourage students to develop a character that is consistent with our divinely graced human nature and our ultimate destiny with God. A wise saying captures this truth:

> Plant an act; reap a habit.
> Plant a habit; reap a virtue or a vice.
> Plant a virtue or a vice; reap a character.
> Plant a character; reap a destiny.

## "Pray It! Study It! Live It!"

*The Catholic Youth Bible* certainly catches the wisdom of the best religious educators in its subtitle, "Pray It! Study It! Live It!" Students have often expressed that they learn the most from classes that allow them to connect the content with life experience. They want "real-life" applications in the midst of studying the material. Students also wonder how prayer and God enter into the moral dilemmas of their life. The cases in this book weave real-life applications with content and prayer through a process for making decisions.

# The LISTEN Process

Moral decision-making skills can be taught. The LISTEN process is the vehicle for these skills. LISTEN is an acronym that outlines the steps in a decision-making process:

**L**ook for the facts.

**I**magine possibilities.

**S**eek insight beyond your own.

**T**urn inward.

**E**xpect God's help.

**N**ame your decision.

As young people learn the steps of the process and study related concepts, the LISTEN process allows for real-life application. Here, too, young people will learn that decision making is both a skill and an art.

The cases in this book are the real-life experiences of real people who have faced moral decisions. Reading the stories of these individuals and then applying the LISTEN process allows teens to explore moral dilemmas from another person's viewpoint.

# Special Features of This Leader's Guide

This guide is designed to be a resource for the *Growing in Christian Morality* textbook (Winona, MN: Saint Mary's Press, 2002), although it can work well with any morality course, parish religious education program, or youth ministry program. Everything that you need to lead a session is provided in a friendly format that puts all relevant information at your fingertips.

The guide also gives you permission to photocopy handouts, cases, and prayer experiences—all of which can be used to build lessons or programs of varied lengths. This guide can also be used in conjunction with the student casebook that has all the cases and LISTEN application pieces in a bound format.

Special features of the leader's guide include the following:

- *a concise introduction* to the LISTEN process, sample questions for each step of the process, and an attractive two-page visual for case applications
- *over thirty cases* divided into themes based on the moral virtues of wise judgment, justice, courage, wholeness, honesty, respect for people, compassion, respect for creation, reverence for life, and peacemaking
- *ten discussion-starters*—a new and creative one for each theme—to help you process the cases
- *ten reproducible handouts* with a short prayer focus based on each of the moral virtues or themes

- *strategies for faith application* to take the concepts out of the learning environment and apply them to the real world
- *an outline of important concepts* to develop for each case, along with a specific focus for each case
- references to the *Catechism of the Catholic Church,* provided as helpful teaching background
- Scripture connections to articles in *The Catholic Youth Bible*
- course connections to relevant topics in the student text *Growing in Christian Morality*
- *case research leads* with relevant Web sites that pertain to concepts, organizations, or issues in the case
- *follow-up to the cases,* when applicable
- *sample questions* for each step of the LISTEN process

## How to Use This Guide

The student casebook and leader's guide are intended to support a morality course by providing meaningful applications of the content. The cases may be used as discussion-starters, assigned as homework for individual reflection, or compiled by students into a decision-making portfolio.

The themes, which are based on the moral virtues, do not need to be studied in any special order, which provides flexibility. Also, depending on the needs of the youth in your class or program, you may choose to study all the cases in a particular theme or just a select few. Because each case has a particular focus, they can stand alone or be used in a more comprehensive program.

At the beginning of each theme section, a short focusing prayer and a suggested discussion-starter help you set the theme. After studying the cases in each theme section, you can follow through further by using the suggested action steps for faith application. The goal here is to truly pray, study, and live the virtue emphasized in each case.

## Ongoing Support

Saint Mary's Press is committed to providing excellent resources for those ministering to youth. One such resource is the Faith Community Builders Web site, *www.smp.org/hs.* This site is filled with resources, links, and discussion related to the study of morality and to the cases presented here.

# WISE JUDGMENT

### Good-Conscience-in-Action

# Theme Section Resources

## Discussion-Starter: Character Role in a Fishbowl

*Vary the way you discuss and process the cases in your classroom. Try this idea during one of the cases in this section.*

Ask for volunteers to participate in a fishbowl discussion, where a small group of students sits in the center or front of class, and has a "normal" discussion while the rest of the class listens. What makes this discussion different is that the students will assume the role of the people in the story and answer questions from those people's perspective. Ask questions that require the students to apply the LISTEN process, such as those in the casebook, or use the statements listed in the concept focus sections. After a good deal of discussion in the fishbowl format, ask the rest of the class to analyze the responses from the "characters."

## Faith Application

After discussing the cases in this theme section, ask the students to consider an action step that would move what they have learned out into the world. Consider these possibilities:

- discussing with the seniors of the school "fun" pranks as opposed to those that vandalize property and hurt people
- learning more about gun control legislation

## Opening Prayer

*(See handout on next page.)*

# A Prayer for Wise Judgment

*Leader:* God of wisdom, let us be open to what you can teach us! Let us hear the words from the eighth chapter of Proverbs that can guide our steps and actions each day.

*Reader 1:* "Does not wisdom call, and does not understanding raise her voice?" (v. 1)

*Reader 2:* "To you, O people, I call, and my cry is to all that live. O simple ones, learn prudence; acquire intelligence, you who lack it." (v. 4)

*Reader 1:* "Hear, for I will speak noble things, and from my lips will come what is right; for my mouth will utter truth." (v. 6–7)

*Reader 3:* "Take my instruction instead of silver, and knowledge rather than choice gold; for wisdom is better than jewels, and all that you may desire cannot compare with her." (v. 10–11)

*Reader 1:* "The fear of the LORD is hatred of evil." (v. 13)

*Reader 4:* "Pride and arrogance and the way of evil and perverted speech I hate." (v. 13)

*Reader 1:* "I have good advice and sound wisdom; I have insight, I have strength." (v. 14)

*Reader 5:* "Those who seek me diligently find me." (v. 17)

*All:* I walk in the way of righteousness, along the paths of justice. Amen.

# Resources for Judgment Case 1

## A Deadly Practical Joke

### Concept Focus: Impulse Control

Throughout the discussion of the case, bring up the following points and have the students apply and reflect on them:

- We practice wise judgment when we develop our *conscience,* make decisions according to it, and carry out those decisions.
- We practice wise judgment when we seek reality by searching for solid information and weighing the *consequences* of each *option.*
- We practice wise judgment when we evaluate the *means* used to accomplish a good end.

### *Catechism* Connections

Read the following passages in the *Catechism* and ask the students to explain how the faith statement can be applied to this case:

- Circumstances are secondary elements of a moral act. (no. 1754)
- We cannot judge the morality of an act by considering only the intention. (no. 1756)
- Willfully damaging private or public property is contrary to moral law. (no. 2409)

### Scripture Connections

*The Catholic Youth Bible* (Winona, MN: Saint Mary's Press) includes an article on responsibility that can connect with Matilda's story:

- "Caught Up in the Moment" (see Ex 32.1–35)

### Course Connections

This case can be used with the course *Growing in Christian Morality* with the chapter on wise judgment:

- knowing one's own feelings and motives (p. 97)

### Follow-up for Judgment Case 1: A Deadly Practical Joke

No charges were filed against Mr. Crabtree.

# The LISTEN Process Applied

Use the sample questions below to help the students work through the application of the LISTEN process for this case. You may wish to suggest questions for the students or focus on one particular section of the process.

## Look for the Facts

1. What was the critical decision Matilda needed to make?
2. What was the critical decision Mr. Crabtree needed to make?
3. What circumstances surrounded the decision?
4. What role did time play in this situation?

## Imagine Possibilities

1. What possible decisions could Matilda have made that night?
2. What possible options did Mr. Crabtree have for handling the situation?
3. What short- and long-term consequences could potentially result from each decision? (You may wish to use the consequence tree handout on page 208 for this activity.)

## Seek Insight Beyond Your Own

1. What would you say to Matilda's suggestion to go back to her house and play a joke on her parents?
2. Who would you turn to for advice in deciding whether or not to play a practical joke on someone?
3. What would your parents expect from you in a situation like this?

## Turn Inward

1. What motives would you have for participating in a practical joke?
2. What role would your conscience play in deciding whether to play a practical joke on someone?
3. How would you feel if someone played a practical joke like this on you?

## Expect God's Help

1. Compose a prayer that would help you make a wise decision in this case.

## Name Your Decision

1. What decision would you make if you were in Matilda's situation?
2. What core values are being upheld in living out that decision?

### Final Questions and Thoughts on Judgment Case 1:
### A Deadly Practical Joke

1. Whom do you most identify with in this case? Why?
2. Apply the LISTEN process from the viewpoint of Mr. Crabtree. How would you handle a situation in which you thought someone had broken into your house?
3. Explain how the virtue of wise judgment was not clearly demonstrated in this case.
4. What does this case teach about impulse control?
5. What lingering questions or thoughts do you have after reflecting on this case?

## A Deadly Practical Joke

One Saturday night, fourteen-year-old Matilda Kaye Crabtree had planned to spend the night at a friend's house while her parents were away. But later she changed her mind and the two girls went back to Matilda's house.

Hours later, around 1:00 a.m., Matilda heard her parents' car pull into the driveway. She and her friend decided to play a practical joke on them by making noises as they hid in a closet. They wanted to make it seem like someone was breaking in.

When Mr. Crabtree heard the noises, he found his gun and went through the house to investigate. Matilda heard her dad approaching and then jumped out of the closet yelling, "Boo!" Taken by surprise, Mr. Crabtree fired his pistol, shooting his daughter in the neck. Matilda's friend was not hurt.

Matilda was rushed to the hospital, where she died twelve hours after the shooting. The last words she spoke to her father were, "I love you, Daddy."

No charges were filed against the father. A deputy said that Mr. Crabtree totally focused on Matilda while she was in the hospital and was devastated by what happened.

## Applying the LISTEN Process

Direct the students to their casebook or photocopy and distribute the LISTEN process handout on page 209 for use with the students.

# Resources for Judgment Case 2

## Stop-Sign Prank

### Concept Focus: Peer Pressure, When to Correct a Friend

Throughout the discussion of the case, bring up the following points and have the students apply and reflect on them:
- We practice wise judgment when we develop our *conscience,* make decisions according to it, and carry out those decisions.
- We practice wise judgment when we evaluate the *means* used to accomplish a good *end.*
- We often have a mixture of motives for what we want to do. Some of them are good, legitimate reasons. But when our reasons are not so admirable, or when we are frightened or angry, we may come up with *rationalizations.* These are attempts to trick ourselves and others into believing that we are doing something for good reasons when we really are not.

### *Catechism* Connections

Read the following passages in the *Catechism,* and ask the students to explain how the faith statements can be applied to this case:
- Circumstances are secondary elements of a moral act. (no. 1754)
- Intention is not the primary focus when judging the morality of an act. (no. 1756)
- We must take responsibility for the sins of others when we take part in the sins too. (no. 1868)

### Scripture Connections

*The Catholic Youth Bible* includes articles on responsibility that relate well to this case:
- "Taking Responsibility" (see Sir 15.11–20)
- "Individuals Are Responsible for Their Behavior!" (see Ezek 18.1–32)

### Course Connections

This case can be used with the course *Growing in Christian Morality* with the chapter on wise judgment:
- knowing one's own feelings and motives (p. 97)
- fooling ourselves with rationalizations (p. 105)
- life and death decisions (p. 106)

## Research for Judgment Case 2: Stop-Sign Prank

Stealing road signs is a common occurrence in the United States. The Federal Highway Administration estimates that one in every ten road signs is vandalized in this country. This is at a cost to taxpayers of over one hundred million dollars.

## Follow-up for Judgment Case 2: Stop-Sign Prank

Parents of the young people killed in the accident in this case had different opinions about what should happen to the persons charged with taking down the stop signs.

One mother of a crash victim, Ann Hertle, said: "They don't deserve to go to jail for fifteeen years. These kids are not hardened criminals, okay? They're just like any of our kids out there on the street right now that we feel are good kids. [They] did something wrong one night. And I don't think their whole lives have to be ruined because of it."

Kevin's parents, June and Les Farr, believe that the intent does not matter; the punishment must fit the crime. "They're convicted killers walking the streets," said Les Farr. "They're not vandals. They're not pranksters."

# The LISTEN Process Applied

Use the questions below to help the students work through the application of the LISTEN process for this case. You may wish to suggest questions for the students or focus on one particular step of the process.

## Look for the Facts

1. What are the key facts of this case?
2. What would be important to know in making the decision whether to participate in pulling up stop signs?

## Imagine Possibilities

1. What are the basic choices that could be made in this situation?
2. What short- and long-term consequences are involved in taking down stop signs? (You may wish to use the consequence tree handout on page 208 for this activity.)
3. What is the most loving response to make in this situation? Why?
4. What are other ways to have fun with your friends besides getting involved in this type of vandalism?

## Seek Insight Beyond Your Own

1. What advice would your family give you in deciding what to do in this case?
2. What advice could you expect from your friends?
3. Is there a legal issue involved in this case?
4. What guidance could be found in examining the Ten Commandments?

## Turn Inward

1. What motive could there be for removing stop signs from the road?
2. From a gut level, what do you think about this situation? Why?
3. What would be most important to you when deciding whether to participate in this prank?
4. What feelings are strongest within you after you read this case?

## Expect God's Help

1. Read Sirach 15:11–20. How might that Scripture reading comfort and challenge you if you were making decisions like the ones in this case?
2. Compose a prayer that you would offer for teens who often find themselves in the company of friends who seek out mischief.

## Name Your Decision

1. Would you decide to participate in taking down stop signs with your friends?
2. What core values are being upheld in living out that decision?

## Final Questions and Thoughts on Judgment Case 2: Stop-Sign Prank

1. What guidelines would you suggest for people who enjoy practical jokes? When do you know that a line has been crossed and that the prank is no longer good-natured?
2. Whom do you most identify with in this case? Why?
3. What lingering questions or thoughts do you have after reflecting on this case?

# Judgment Case 2

## Stop-Sign Prank

After bowling in a Wednesday night league, Kevin left the bowling alley to meet up with two friends and go cruising. They were driving on a dark stretch of highway outside Tampa, Florida. They passed a sign warning that a stop sign was ahead, but the sign wasn't visible. The boys drove into the intersection without stopping and were hit by an eight-ton semi-truck. The car left no skid marks, and the prosecutor said that the boys did not see the truck coming. All three boys were killed by the tremendous impact.

The police investigation found that the stop sign had been pulled from the ground and was left lying on the side of the road where no driver could see it. Kevin's mother could not believe that anyone could do something like this to deliberately put people in danger.

Three people were suspected of removing the stop sign and consequently causing the accident. Three roommates, Thomas Miller, Christopher Cole, and Nissa Bailey, were heard bragging to friends and reporters about vandalizing road signs and drinking heavily. One reporter asked Christopher why he would do something like that. "Just for a rush," he said. "I don't really think it was a rush like a happy rush. It was more like a 'I hope we don't get caught' type of rush. It was, in certain ways, fun."

Christopher and Nissa also confessed to police that they dumped some of the stolen signs into a creek. The three admitted that they took down nineteen signs, but not the one that caused Kevin's fatal accident. Nissa said, "I'm sorry to the parents that their kids got killed, but I know in my heart I didn't do it."

When asked by a reporter if they had thought about what might happen when taking the stop signs, Christopher Cole simply said, "We didn't think it through at the time." Nissa said, "We didn't expect all of this out of just taking a few signs off of back roads."

"People may look at them and say, 'Oh, it's just a prank,' but the bottom line is, these people have to be held accountable for a prank that resulted in the death of three people," said the reporter. Charged with grand theft and manslaughter, Thomas Miller, Christopher Cole, and Nissa Bailey were all found guilty. The jury decided upon this verdict in less than four hours.

## Applying the LISTEN Process

Direct the students to their casebook or photocopy and distribute the LISTEN process handout on page 209 for use with the students.

**Resources for Judgment Case 3**

## A Senior Prank Gone Too Far?

### Concept Focus: Foreseeing Consequences

Throughout the discussion of the case, bring up the following points and have the students apply and reflect on them:

- To see reality clearly is to seek out solid information and to weigh the *consequences* of each option.
- The virtue of wise judgment involves the ability to evaluate the *means* used to accomplish a good end.
- The habit of wise judgment moves us away from *rationalizing.* Instead we begin to acknowledge what truly motivates us, even when we are not proud of our motives.

### *Catechism* Connections

Read the following passages in the *Catechism,* and ask the students to explain how the faith statements can be applied to this case:

- The morality of an action depends on the act, intentions, and circumstances. (no. 1750)
- Intention is not the primary focus when judging the morality of an act. (no. 1756)
- Children should obey the reasonable directives of their teachers and of those to whom their parents have entrusted them. (no. 2217)

### Scripture Connections

*The Catholic Youth Bible* includes the following article on responsibility that is relevant to this case:

- "Irresponsible Children" (see Ezek 23.1–21)

### Course Connections

This case can be used with the course *Growing in Christian Morality* with the chapter on wise judgment:

- seeing reality clearly (p. 95)
- knowing one's own feelings and motives (p. 97)
- sticky situations (p. 103)
- fooling ourselves with rationalizations (p. 105)

## Research for Judgment Case 3: A Senior Prank Gone Too Far?

While school vandalism has declined in recent years, senior pranks have become more destructive. Many students consider senior pranks to be "rites of passage." But according to Michael Carr, a spokesman for the National Association of Secondary School Principals: "Each year, it escalates. Someone wants to top someone else." A possible motivation for the escalating destruction comes from students wanting to see their deeds on the evening news.

Some of the worst incidents have included

- fires causing over ten million dollars in damage at two schools
- spray-painting school property
- putting bleach on an athletic field and defacing the scoreboard
- tossing fire bombs through windows

"At one point, you called them senior pranks, but I don't call these things senior pranks," said Mr. Carr. "These are individual students getting out of control."

# The LISTEN Process Applied

Use the sample questions below to help the students work through the application of the LISTEN process for this case. You may wish to suggest questions for the students or focus on one particular section of the process.

## Look for the Facts

1. Why is a senior prank being planned?
2. What facts would you want to know in order to make a decision about whether to take part in the senior prank?

## Imagine Possibilities

1. What are all the possible senior pranks that you can think of that would be good-natured and fun for all involved?
2. What advantages and disadvantages do you see in each brainstormed prank? (You may wish to use the consequence tree handout on page 208 for this activity.)
3. How can your creativity be employed in this situation?
4. What potential problems can you identify for the pranks planned in this case—specifically the foam-rubber balls and the release of rodents?

## Seek Insight Beyond Your Own

1. What advice would your parents give you about being involved in the senior prank?
2. What would most of your friends advise you to do in this case?
3. Are there any legal issues involved in the pranks planned in this case?
4. What values found in the Ten Commandments could provide guidance in this case? Explain fully.

## Turn Inward

1. What does your conscience tell you about the foam-rubber ball prank?
2. What does your conscience say about the mice, rats, and crickets released in the hall?
3. What would motivate someone to come up with these pranks and take part in them? Do you understand these motives?
4. What feelings do you have about these pranks?

## Expect God's Help

1. Read the following Scripture passages and explain how the readings could provide guidance and challenge if you were making the decision whether to be involved in the prank.
   - Proverbs 15:22
   - Proverbs 16:1–2
   - Proverbs 23:19
   - Proverbs 26:18–19
   - Proverbs 30:32

## Name Your Decision

1. What decision would you make about participating in the senior pranks?
2. What core values are being upheld in living out that decision?

### Final Questions and Thoughts on Judgment Case 3: A Senior Prank Gone Too Far?

- What would be a suitable consequence for being involved in this senior prank? Why?
- Does your school have any guidelines for senior pranks?
- What types of expectations would you suggest to an administration of a high school and a senior class?
- Whom do you most identify with in this case? Why?
- What lingering questions or thoughts do you have after reflecting on this case?

## A Senior Prank Gone Too Far?

Danielle Faustini came up with an idea for Senior Prank Day at Pascack Hills High School: Seniors would throw five thousand foam-rubber balls down the hallways. For three months, she and many seniors raised money to buy the balls. Danielle's mother and father were aware that she was planning the prank and told her that she may suffer consequences if she were caught by the school.

After the five thousand balls were unleashed on Senior Prank Day, the pranks began to escalate. Some students released mice, rats, and crickets into the halls. When students heard that a classmate was being punished, dozens staged a walkout and someone pulled the fire alarms.

Chaos filled the halls as students ran screaming throughout the school. The principal of the school, Manuel Ferreira, collapsed during the pranks and was rushed to the hospital for an emergency angioplasty.

Jeanine Falinski, a senior, admitted that she was part of the rubber balls prank and turned herself in to school administration. "It was an innocent joke to throw the balls, and some people took it out of control," she said. Jeanine was not suspended for her part in the prank. She noted: "The suspensions were very random. Someone who did the same thing I did got four days. This is all a joke."

The acting superintendent noted that some seniors were punished by not being allowed to go on a rafting trip or to the senior prom, and some would not be allowed to attend graduation. He said: "We don't view what happened as a lark. This could have been dangerous."

A police detective noted that the students could be charged with three offenses: setting off false fire alarms, abusing animals, and inciting a riot (a stampede occurred after the animals were released in a crowded hallway).

The school board president also pointed out that the incident was very serious. "People could have gotten seriously hurt," she said. "I'm grateful to God that no one was."

Danielle Faustini was suspended for four days. Her mother was outraged by the punishment. She acknowledged that her daughter and others felt badly that the principal was rushed to the hospital, but "on the other hand, they weren't really ultimately responsible for that situation." As far as the prank itself, Danielle's mom said: "I thought it was just kind of a fun thing. It was all in jest."

## Applying the LISTEN Process

Direct the students to their casebook or photocopy and distribute the LISTEN process handout on page 209 for use with the students.

# JUSTICE
Love's Minimum

### Discussion-Starter: Point-Counterpoint

*Vary the way you discuss and process the cases in your classroom. Try this idea during one of the cases in this section.*

Hand out two index cards to each student. Ask the students to list on one of the cards one positive point they found in reading over the case. Ask them to write down a counterpoint, something that may have a negative effect or consequence in the case, on the other card. Using a board or wall at the front of the room, write the words *point* and *counterpoint* on separate sides. Instruct the students to come up one at a time, read their cards aloud to the class, and then tape them on the appropriate side.

Encourage the students to listen carefully throughout the process. When all the cards are placed, ask the students which side was more convincing and why. It may also be helpful to categorize the points-counterpoints and discover the key elements of the case as determined by the students.

## Faith Application

After discussing the cases in this theme section, ask the students to consider an action step that would move what they have learned out into the world. Consider these possibilities:

- Read more about civil-action suits against large companies. Rent the movie, *A Civil Action* (1998, PG-13, 112 minutes) to stimulate discussion. The movie focuses on a leather production company that is sued by a group of families who believe the contaminated areas caused the leukemia that resulted in the deaths of their loved ones. Consider inviting a lawyer to speak to the class about these class-action lawsuits. Encourage the lawyer to talk about how justice can take place in the legal system.

- Research sexual harassment guidelines in high school handbooks in your area. Contact your representatives to find out about any legislation in this area that may be coming up for discussion or vote.

- Work with a group of students to curtail any vandalism (graffiti, for example) that may take place in your school or city. Develop an action plan that may include clean up as well as education.

## Opening Prayer

*(See handout on next page.)*

# A Prayer for Justice

*Leader:* Let justice fill our hearts, enlighten our minds, be shown in our
    actions, and spread like sunshine!

*All:* Justice-minded people

*Reader 1:* speak the truth

*Reader 2:* in places of power.

*All:* Justice-minded people

*Reader 3:* work to understand

*Reader 4:* the question: Why is this happening?

*All:* Justice-minded people

*Reader 5:* commit themselves

*Reader 6:* to living the Gospel.

*All:* Justice-minded people

*Reader 7:* know Christ's lessons in the Beatitudes

*Reader 8:* and *become* those attitudes in the world.

*All:* Loving God of justice, as we answer the questions of who we are
    becoming and who we'd like to become, let us continually reflect on
    how the virtue of justice can be lived out in our decisions. May we
    work to bring forth the reign of your justice! Amen.

## Concept Focus: Rights, Common Good, Injustice

Throughout the discussion of the case, bring up the following points and have the students apply and reflect on them:

- We practice justice when we strive to ensure the well-being of ourself and others. Our relationships must first be just if they are to be loving. That is what Pope Paul IV meant when he called justice "love's minimum."
- *Social justice* obliges us to contribute to the *common good,* the condition of the social whole that enables all human beings to flourish. Social justice can be accomplished by respecting the needs of everyone in group decisions, by serving in community projects, and by avoiding harmful actions such as vandalizing property or monopolizing resources for oneself, one's group, or one's generation.
- *Distributive justice* organizes social systems and society for the common good. Governments and private businesses are obliged to create structures in which burdens and benefits are shared and distributed fairly.

## *Catechism* Connections

Read the following passages in the *Catechism,* and ask the students to explain how the faith statements can be applied to this case:

- Justice means giving what is due to God and neighbor. (no. 1807)
- Those who have authority should exercise it as a service. (no. 2235)
- Authority must be practiced justly and responsibly. (no. 2236)
- We must respect the integrity of creation. (no. 2415)

## Scripture Connections

*The Catholic Youth Bible* includes articles on justice that connect with the concepts of this case:

- "I Therefore Commit" (see Hos 12.2–6)
- "What Goes Around" (see Obadiah, verse 15)
- "Rethinking Social Structures" (see Philemon, verses 8–21)

## Course Connections

This case can be used with the course *Growing in Christian Morality* with the chapter on justice:
- actions of the avoiders (p. 109)
- rights and obligations (p. 112)
- distributive justice (p. 125)
- using your power (p. 131)

## Research for Justice Case 1: Blowing the Whistle

You can pursue further research on this topic by searching Web sites that serve the National Cancer Institute or W. R. Grace & Company or by logging on to our Faith Community Builders Web site, *www.smp.org/bs,* and searching the links and resources provided there.

# LISTEN Process Applied

Use the sample questions below to help the students work through the application of the LISTEN process for this case. You may wish to suggest questions for the students or focus on one particular section of the process.

## Look for the Facts

1. What are the most important facts in this case?
2. What connections did Gayla make between her parents' illness, the asbestos mine, and the W. R. Grace company?
3. What critical information would you want to know before making a decision to hold the company liable?

## Imagine Possibilities

1. What options did Gayla have for dealing with the deaths of innocent people and the environment?
2. What would happen if Gayla chose to do nothing?
3. What short- and long-term consequences did Gayla face by going up against a large company? (You may wish to use the consequence tree handout on page 208 for this activity.)
4. How could Gayla have used creativity in these choices? Explain.

## Seek Insight Beyond Your Own

1. Would your family and friends advise you to pursue the legal end of justice?
2. Where did Gayla seek insight for her decision?

## Turn Inward

1. What are your feelings about this case?
2. What would your motives be for going up against a large corporation?
3. What would your conscience tell you to do in this case?

## Expect God's Help

1. Compose a prayer that you would pray if you were Gayla.
2. Read 1 Samuel 17. How might the story of David and Goliath comfort and challenge you if you were making decisions like the ones in this case?

## Name Your Decision

1. What decision would you make if you were in Gayla's shoes? Why?
2. What core values are being upheld in living out that decision?

## Final Questions and Thoughts on Justice Case 1: Blowing the Whistle

1. Whom do you most identify with in this case? Why?
2. How should these environmental issues with large companies be handled?
3. What lingering questions or thoughts do you have after reflecting on this case?

## Blowing the Whistle

Gayla Benefield's father took a job working at an open-pit asbestos mine on Zonolite Mountain, near Libby, Montana, when Gayla was ten years old. Her father had been unemployed, and Gayla remembers that summer being a happy one because he got the mining job.

About thirteen years later, it was discovered that Perley Vatland, Gayla's dad, had severe lung problems, later diagnosed as advanced asbestosis. Eight years later he died from the disease that slowly cuts off the ability to breathe. Gayla's mother was eventually diagnosed with the same disease, dying at the age of seventy-nine. Gayla describes her death as a "slow suffocation."

Gayla discovered that it was not only her parents but hundreds of other residents of her town who were killed or made sick by the asbestos. Some were miners, but others were victims of the dust that came home on the clothes and shoes of their loved ones.

W. R. Grace & Company, based in Columbia, Maryland, owned the mines for over thirty years before shutting them down in 1990. Gayla believes that the company knew for years about the dangers of asbestos exposure but did little to eliminate them. She and others have fought the company in the courts since the late 1980s. In 1998 Gayla won a $250,000 settlement for the wrongful death of her mother. This was a very important case since it was the first fatality from the town of Libby that was attributed to secondhand asbestos exposure.

Gayla did not quit there, however. A year later she noticed that an area close to the old mine site had residue from the unused ore that was dense with asbestos. "The whole road was sparkly with vermiculite," she said. "I was absolutely, totally shocked."

She was later outraged when she came to find out that W. R. Grace was about to collect money from the state for cleaning up the area. New grass and trees were planted, but the asbestos residue remained. Gayla filed a complaint, and regional newspapers got involved and investigated. Documentation was found for at least eighty-eight local deaths caused by the asbestos exposure. The publicity got the U.S. Environmental Protection Agency (EPA) involved in a $14.5 million federal cleanup and screening project.

The EPA's tests have not pointed clearly in one direction. According to the EPA on-site coordinator, Paul Peronard: "As far as houses, we don't have a clean bill of health. But we don't have any obvious problems."

W. R. Grace insists that it has completed the cleanup required by the state. The company also believes that the workers and families who got sick were contaminated before Grace bought the mine or in the first years after that. Little was known about asbestos dangers at that point. The EPA and W. R. Grace are working to clean up the milling and shipping facilities, although there is disagreement about how much the company should do.

Going door to door, Gayla has worked to encourage sick mineworkers and survivors to sue W. R. Grace. Over 187 civil actions have been filed against the company. One-third of the actions were settled out of court, and two-thirds of the actions are still pending.

People are always asking Gayla why she did not leave her hometown after she found out what was wrong. She replied: "I've lived here too long to just turn around and leave. It's my home. I feel responsible for it."

## Applying the LISTEN Process

Direct the students to their casebook or photocopy and distribute the LISTEN process handout on page 209 for use with the students.

## Harassment at School

### Concept Focus: Rights, Dignity, Sexual Harassment

Throughout the discussion of the case, bring up the following points and have the students apply and reflect on them:

- Justice strives to ensure the well-being of everyone. Our relationships must first be just if they are to be loving. That is what Pope Paul IV meant when he called justice "love's minimum."
- *Individual justice* focuses on the obligation that we have to another because of a relationship we have by contract, deal, family ties, friendship, and so on.
- *Distributive justice* organizes social systems and society for the common good. Governments and private businesses are obliged to create structures in which burdens and benefits are shared and distributed fairly among the people.

### *Catechism* Connections

Read the following passages in the *Catechism,* and ask the students to explain how the faith statements can be applied to this case:

- Equality rests in our dignity as people made in God's image. (no. 1935)
- Everyone enjoys a natural right to respect; unjust injury to reputation is an offense against dignity and charity. (nos. 2477 and 2479)

### Scripture Connections

*The Catholic Youth Bible* includes articles that connect to this case:

- "Betrayed!" (see Psalm 55)
- "Doing the Right Thing" (see 1 Thess 2.1–2)

### Course Connections

This case can be used with the course *Growing in Christian Morality* with the chapter on justice:

- basic rights and well-being (p. 112)
- using your power (p. 131)

## Research for Justice Case 2: Harassment at School

Sexual harassment is a problem in our society. A 1996 University of Michigan study found that 83 percent of teenage girls and 60 percent of teenage boys claimed that they had been sexually harassed. The definition of sexual harassment ranged from touching to being "mooned." The study also showed that over 50 percent of those surveyed admitted to harassing other people.

You can pursue further research by searching Web sites on the topic of sexual harassment or by logging on to our Faith Community Builders Web site, *www.smp.org/bs,* and searching the links and resources provided there.

# The LISTEN Process Applied

Use the sample questions below to help the students work through the application of the LISTEN process for this case. You may wish to suggest questions for the students or focus on one particular section of the process.

## Look for the Facts

1. What are the facts surrounding Coren's experiences with Mark, teachers, friends, and school?
2. What is sexual harassment?

## Imagine Possibilities

1. What are all the possible ways Coren could have handled this situation?
2. What short- and long-term consequences would be involved with each possible option? Why? (You may wish to use the consequence tree handout on page 208 for this activity.)

## Seek Insight Beyond Your Own

1. What advice would your friends give you if you were in Coren's situation?
2. What would your family encourage you to do about the situation?
3. What does the law say about sexual harassment? What options does the legal system afford Coren for dealing with the situation?
4. What guidelines would your school have for behavior like Mark's?
5. What advice for Coren can be found in reading the Beatitudes?

## Turn Inward

1. If you were in Coren's situation, would you have an intuitive understanding of the situation? How would your "gut" influence how you would act upon these experiences?
2. What would hold you back from confronting Mark?
3. What would your motives be for filing a complaint with the school?
4. What feelings would you have regarding your teacher and school if your teacher made a comment like the one Coren's teacher made?

## Expect God's Help

1. Compose a prayer that you would pray if you were Coren.
2. Compose a prayer you would say for Mark.
3. Read Psalm 3. How might that Scripture reading comfort and challenge you if you were in Coren's situation?

## Name Your Decision

1. How would you decide to handle this situation if you were Coren?
2. What core values are being upheld in living out that decision?

### Final Questions and Thoughts on Justice Case 2: Harassment at School

1. Do you identify with Coren in this case? Why or why not?
2. What do you think was going on with Mark? Why would he say those things to Coren?
3. Was the teacher's comment appropriate? How could the teacher have handled the situation differently? Are there any guidelines at your school regarding sexual harassment?
4. What lingering questions or thoughts do you have after reflecting on this case?

# Justice Case 2

## Harassment at School

Coren Cooper's mom always told her not to be ashamed of her developing body. As she developed more fully, Coren remained positive and confident, especially with her mother's encouragement.

One day in sophomore biology class, a boy named Mark called out her name. When she turned around, everyone started laughing. Coren did not hear what was said, and her friends would not tell her, so she went back to work. A while later, Mark made the comment again and Coren heard it—it was a joke about the size of her breasts. Amidst all the laughter of her peers, Coren felt very uncomfortable and didn't know what to do. She tried to dismiss the comment, acting like it didn't bother her, but deep down she felt anger and hurt and wanted to "knock him out."

The laughter spurred Mark on to make more remarks about Coren's breast size. A few minutes later, Coren asked him to stop, telling him it was not funny. But Mark would not stop. They had known each other for about four years and always got along, so this surprised Coren.

When the teacher came back into the room, Coren told her what happened and the teacher just laughed and said: "Look at what you're wearing. You wear those tight sweaters every day. What do you expect?"

Coren could not believe what her teacher said. Her school had a dress code, and she was wearing jeans, sneakers, and a sweater—nothing inappropriate. When Coren told her friends, they laughed as well. One even said: "Ms. Conner kind of has a point. If you wear tight clothes, you can't be upset when boys make comments."

Coren felt betrayed and alone. For the first time in her life, she felt embarrassed about her body and wondered if she was to blame. She got home and tried to tape her breasts down. She thought that by doing this and by wearing baggy clothes she could take care of the issue.

Coren's mom, who is a teacher herself, was outraged when Coren told her about the incident. She encouraged Coren to file a sexual harassment complaint with the school. The next day Coren was prepared to talk to her counselors but decided against it. In class Mark made more comments about her breast size, so she threatened to report him to the counselor. This made Mark stop for the time being, but later Coren found out that he was spreading rumors of a sexual nature about her. The comments escalated, and Coren almost reached the breaking point.

Coren's friends urged her to see the school counselor, who immediately told her it was not her fault. Mark was called into the office, and he owned up to everything. He apologized to Coren and told her that he did not realize how much he had hurt her. He also thanked her for turning him in. At first Coren did not believe what she heard, but she could see that he was truly sorry.

Coren chose not to file a formal complaint that would stay on Mark's record and not to have him suspended. She decided that his genuine apology was enough. The following year Coren and Mark became friends again. "As horrible as the whole experience was, we both learned a lot from it," Coren said. "I learned that asking for help doesn't mean that you're weak, and Mark learned sexual harassment is no joke—and that inappropriate comments that degrade a person or hurt their feelings shouldn't be laughed off." Coren feels certain that Mark will never treat another girl the way he treated her. This fills her with pride. "Now I know how strong I really am."

## Applying the LISTEN Process

Direct the students to their casebook or photocopy and distribute the LISTEN process handout on page 209 for use with the students.

## Appropriate Punishment, or Torture?

### Concept Focus: Social Injustice, Harming the Common Good

Throughout the discussion of the case, bring up the following points and have the students apply and reflect on them:

- Justice strives to ensure the well-being of everyone. Our relationships must first be just if they are to be loving. That is what Pope Paul IV meant when he called justice "love's minimum."
- *Individual justice* focuses on the obligation that one person has to another because of a relationship they have by contract, deal, family ties, friendship, and so on.
- *Distributive justice* organizes social systems and society for the common good. Governments and private businesses are obliged to create structures in which burdens and benefits are shared and distributed fairly among the people.

### *Catechism* Connections

Read the following passages in the *Catechism,* and ask the students to explain how the faith statements can be applied to this case:

- Torture is contrary to respect for the person and for human dignity. (no. 2297)
- The seventh commandment calls us to respect other's property. (no. 2401)
- There must be reparation for injustice. (no. 2412)

### Scripture Connections

*The Catholic Youth Bible* includes an article on justice that connects with the concept emphasized in this case:

- "What Goes Around" (see Obadiah, verse 15)

### Course Connections

This case can be used with the course *Growing in Christian Morality* with the chapter on justice:

- doing harm to the common good (pp. 122–123)
- victimized by public vandalism (p. 122)

## Research for Justice Case 3:
## Appropriate Punishment, or Torture?

Vandalism destroys public and private property. Find out more about this issue in your community. You can pursue further research on this topic by logging on to our Faith Community Builders Web site, *www.smp.org/hs*, and searching the links and resources provided there.

# The LISTEN Process Applied

Use the sample questions below to help the students work through the application of the LISTEN process for this case. You may wish to suggest questions for the students or focus on one particular section of the process.

## Look for the Facts

1. What critical decisions did Michael face?
2. What critical information would you want to know before making a decision regarding Michael's consequences for spray-painting cars?

## Imagine Possibilities

1. What options did Michael have for enjoying a night out with his friends?
2. What short- and long-term consequences would be associated with each choice? (You may wish to use the consequence tree handout on page 208 for this activity.)
3. How could Michael and his friends have used creativity in their choices? Explain.

## Seek Insight Beyond Your Own

1. Would your friends encourage you to vandalize property?
2. If you lived in another country, how important would it be to find out the laws of the land?
3. What underlying values present in the ninth and tenth commandments could provide guidance for Michael and his friends?

## Turn Inward

1. What are your feelings about this case?
2. What possible motives could there be for vandalizing cars by spray-painting them?
3. What would your conscience tell you to do in this case if you were with Michael and his friends?

## Expect God's Help

1. What would you pray if you were in a foreign jail?
2. Read Ephesians 2:1–5. How would that Scripture reading both challenge and comfort you if you were in Michael's situation?

## Name Your Decision

1. What decision would you make if you were in Michael's situation? Why?
2. What core values upheld in living out that decision?

## Final Questions and Thoughts on Justice Case 3: Appropriate Punishment, or Torture?

1. Whom do you most identify with in this case? Why?
2. What would be an appropriate punishment for Michael?
3. Should a U.S. citizen be immune from the laws of another country when living there?
4. Why does Amnesty International speak out against caning?
5. Do you believe in corporal punishment? Is it an effective way to "teach a lesson"? What lesson would it teach?
6. How is vandalism a social injustice?
7. What lingering questions or thoughts do you have after reflecting on this case?

# Justice Case 3

## Appropriate Punishment, or Torture?

Michael Peter Fay was born in Saint Louis, Missouri, grew up in Dayton, Ohio, and eventually moved to the country of Singapore to live with his mother and stepfather. There he was a normal American teenager who played baseball and football. He was a student at the Singapore American School and a waiter at a Hard Rock Café. He spent his money at discos and liked to go out with his friends.

One night Michael and his friends went wild. They spray-painted and egged cars, and stole street signs.

A few days later, Michael and four others were brought to the principal's office at school, where they were met by police investigators. The investigators went through the students' lockers and eventually searched Michael's home. They found several street signs in Michael's apartment. All the boys were taken to the police department and interrogated harshly. Michael wrote in a statement that after he was grabbed by the hair and slapped in the face he started crying and pleaded for the investigators not to hit him.

Michael was incarcerated and was not allowed an attorney for the first two days of his incarceration. He was allowed to talk to his parents and a U.S. embassy official only once for a very short time. In custody for over a week, Michael was able to smuggle a note to his mother through another teen who was released. In it he wrote: "We sleep on concrete floors, and there are ants all around us. The investigators have tried to get things out of us that we have not done. They have punched, kicked, slapped, and whipped most of us. I'm scared."

Michael claimed that he reached a breaking point and admitted to spray-painting eighteen cars. Prosecutors told him that if he pleaded guilty, his conviction would be lessened to spray-painting two cars, throwing eggs at two other cars, and possessing street signs. Because the spray-paint was easily removed from the cars, Michael's family thought that the judge would give Michael probation. According to his father, the plea bargain was a quick way to get Michael out of jail and back to the U.S. Michael maintained, however, that his confession was coerced.

On his day in court, Michael's defense attorneys told the judge that his behaviors were the pranks of a schoolboy. They pleaded for leniency. They also informed the court that Michael had ADD, attention deficit disorder. The judge dismissed these arguments, however, announcing that Michael would be fined, sentenced to four months in prison, and caned.

Caning involves being struck on the bare buttocks with a four-foot-long, half-inch-thick rattan cane that has been soaked in water so it will not break. The intent is to split the flesh and cause permanent scarring. Amnesty International categorizes caning as torture. Michael's case caused an outcry from many people in the U.S. and from many Americans living in Singapore. President Bill Clinton intervened on Michael's behalf, stating: "We recognize that Singapore has a certain right to enforce their own criminal laws. But we believe that this punishment is extreme, and we hope very much that somehow it will be reconsidered."

All pleas were rejected, and Michael received the caning.

## Applying the LISTEN Process

Direct the students to their casebook, or photocopy and distribute the LISTEN process handout on page 209 for use with the students.

# COURAGE
### Facing Our Fears for the Sake of the Good

# Theme Section Resources

## Discussion-Starter: Chew and Digest

*Vary the way you discuss and process the cases in your classroom. Try this idea during one of the cases in this section.*

Bring enough pieces of taffy, caramels, or Tootsie Rolls for each student to have three. Choose three of the sample LISTEN questions to discuss in large group. You may want to look at the final questions section. Write one question at a time on the overhead, chalkboard, or computer projection device and then read it aloud to the class. Instruct the students to "chew" on some of their ideas for a period of time. They should think about their response to the question while they chew the candy. Once they "digest" the candy, they can raise their hand to share their thoughts with the class. The point of this exercise is to encourage extroverts to think some ideas through before they speak and to give introverts time to process before listening and sharing.

## Faith Application

After discussing the cases in this theme section, ask the students to consider an action step that would move what they have learned out into the world. Consider these possibilities:
- organizing a "Call to Courage" campaign in your school or community that celebrates true heroes and acts of courage
- educating others about AIDS
- hosting a prayer service for those who died in the Holocaust

## Opening Prayer

*(See handout on next page.)*

# A Prayer for Courage

*Leader:* "Be strong, and let your heart take courage, all you who wait for the LORD" (Psalm 31:24).

*Reader 1:* Be with us as we face our fears honestly.

*All:* Be strong and let your heart take courage, all you who wait for the Lord.

*Reader 2:* Be with us when we are threatened with rejection, failure, or harm.

*All:* Be strong and let your heart take courage, all you who wait for the Lord.

*Reader 3:* Loving God, be with us when we are faced with a difficult decision. Guide us to choose the good.

*All:* Be strong and let your heart take courage, all you who wait for the Lord.

*Reader 4:* There are times when we do not feel understood by those who know us and those who don't.

*All:* Be strong and let your heart take courage, all you who wait for the Lord.

*Reader 5:* Be with us when we face the unfamiliar.

*All:* Be strong and let your heart take courage, all you who wait for the Lord.

*Reader 6:* God, let us feel your presence in those times where we feel humiliated or shamed.

*All:* Be strong and let your heart take courage, all you who wait for the Lord.

*Leader:* God of many blessings, we look to the example of your son, Jesus, as we strive to make the wisest decisions with hearts filled with courage. Send your Spirit to guide us this day and always. We ask this in your name. Amen.

# Resources for Courage Case 1

## Rescuing Friendship

### Concept Focus: Choosing to Act for the Good

Throughout the discussion of the case, bring up the following points and have the students apply and reflect on them:
- *Courage* is the ability to do good in the face of harm or threat of injury, whether physical or psychological. Without courage, very little good work would get done.
- We cannot judge the morality of decisions by considering only the intention that causes them.

### *Catechism* Connections

Consider looking up the following passages in the *Catechism*, and ask the students to explain how the faith statements can be applied to this case:
- Fortitude strengthens us. (no. 1808)
- We cannot do evil so that good may result from it. (no. 1756)

### Scripture Connections

*The Catholic Youth Bible* includes articles on courage:
- "Be Not Afraid" (see Josh 1.5–9)
- "Taking On Goliath" (see 1 Samuel, chapter 17)
- "What Makes a Hero?" (see 1 Macc 9.19–22)
- "I Will Sacrifice Myself" (see 2 Maccabees, chapter 7)
- "Courage" (see Psalm 31)
- "Facing Fear" (see Jer 37.11–21)
- "A Courageous Stance" (see Acts 14.1–7)

### Course Connections

This case can be used with the course *Growing in Christian Morality* with the chapter on courage:
- what courage is and is not (pp. 135–137)
- choosing the good (p. 138)
- strategies for taming our fears (p. 148)

## Research for Courage Case 1: Rescuing Friendship

Irene Gut Opdyke saved Jewish people during the Holocaust. You can pursue further research on this topic by searching Web sites for the United States Holocaust Museum or the Simon Wiesenthal Center, or by logging on to our Faith Community Builders Web site, *www.smp.org/bs,* and searching the links and resources provided there.

## Follow-up for Courage Case 1: Rescuing Friendship

- Over fifteen thousand non-Jewish people are honored at Yad Vashem for saving Jewish lives.
- Irene Gut Opdyke coauthored a book about her personal experiences called *Into the Flames: The Life Story of a Righteous Gentile.* Her story is also included in the book called *Courage to Care* by Carol Rittner and Sondra Myers.

# The LISTEN Process Applied

Use the sample questions below to help the students work through the application of the LISTEN process for this case. You may wish to suggest questions for the students or focus on one particular section of the process.

## Look for the Facts

1. What critical decisions did Irene face?
2. Who were the key people involved in this situation?
3. What dangers surrounded Irene during this time?

## Imagine Possibilities

1. What possible decisions could Irene have made in this situation?
2. Name the short- and long-term consequences for each possible choice. (You may wish to use the consequence tree handout on page 208 for this activity.)
3. What would the most loving response be in this situation?
4. Put yourself in the situation of the Jewish people in this story. What are your options?

## Seek Insight Beyond Your Own

1. What advice would Irene find in the Beatitudes?
2. Choosing to hide the Jewish people was against Nazi law. What issues were involved by choosing to break this law? How would you decide whether something legal is moral?
3. What would your family and friends advise you to do if you were in Irene's situation?
4. What guidance does the church offer regarding situations like Irene's?

## Turn Inward

1. How would your conscience guide you in making this decision?
2. What feelings do you believe you would experience if you were in Irene's situation?
3. How would you judge the personal debasement of forced sex in Irene's situation?
4. What feelings do you imagine you would have if you were a person in hiding?
5. What motives would you have had for hiding your Jewish friends? What would have motivated you not to hide them?

## Expect God's Help

1. Compose a prayer that you would pray if you were Irene.
2. Compose a prayer that you would say if you were one of the Jewish people in hiding.
3. Read Psalm 61. How might that Scripture reading comfort and challenge you if you were in Irene's situation?

## Name Your Decision

1. What decision would you make? Why?
2. What core values are being upheld in living out that decision?

### Final Questions and Thoughts on Courage Case 1: Rescuing Friendship

1. Whom do you most identify with in this case? Why?
2. What lingering questions or thoughts do you have after reflecting on this case?
3. Discuss with the students a quote from Irene Gut Opdyke:

   Hate breeds hate and love can bring wonderful results. Learn from each other, regardless of race or creed. Only you can build something for the future. The skinheads, the KKK, the hate-mongers—they are the losers and you are not.

4. What role did the Catholic church play in speaking out against the injustices of the Holocaust?

# Courage Case 1

## Rescuing Friendship

Irene Gut Opdyke was a seventeen-year-old nursing student when the Germans defeated the Polish army in 1939. With some other nurses and a group of Polish soldiers, she fled to the east to escape the Germans. Irene eventually ended up in a Ukranian forest where Russian soldiers beat and gang-raped her, then left her for dead. Another soldier found her barely alive and took her to a hospital where she recovered and began working.

Two years later, Irene went back to Poland to find her family. On the way, she was captured by Germans. She was forced to work for a time in a munitions plant and then as a waitress in a dining hall for German officers. One November day as she folded napkins and set out silverware, Irene witnessed firsthand the cruel brutality of the Nazis. She saw a young SS officer pull a baby from its mother's arms, toss it in the air, and shoot it like a bird.

"I could only say, 'Oh God, my God, where are you?'" After praying that night, Irene remembered: "In the morning, for some reason, there was an answer in my soul, in my heart. That God gave us free will to be good or bad, and it's up to us."

Irene was eventually assigned to work for the local commander of the Gestapo. At his villa she came to supervise twelve Jewish slave laborers who did laundry for the Germans. In time, Irene became good friends with them.

"I did not think of them as different because they were Jews," Irene said. "To me, we were all in trouble and we had a common enemy."

Irene stole food and left it for the Jewish workers. When she overheard high-ranking Nazi officers planning raids of the nearby ghetto, Irene passed on the information to the twelve laborers. Lives were saved because the twelve then passed that information to the ghetto.

When the time came for the ghetto to be liquidated and the Jewish people to be sent to death camps, Irene hid her twelve friends in the villa where she worked. This was very difficult because one of the twelve became pregnant. It was also a terrifying time because discovery would mean certain death for the twelve and her.

Irene was constantly reminded of the possibility that they could all die. One day she was forced to watch the hanging of a Christian family that tried to help a Jewish family. The Nazis hung the children first. "The children were screaming. And not only this, the horrible noise when they tried to breathe. I closed my eyes. I could not see it. But you see even with the closed eyes because you hear. And that was that day that I went to the villa like a zombie."

The same day as the hanging, Irene forgot to lock the door where she was hiding her Jewish friends, and the commander discovered them.

Irene begged him to let them live. He went into his office to think and later came out, telling her that he would keep her secret if she became his mistress. Irene decided to yield to his demand.

"I could not tell my friends what I was doing," she said. "How could you tell them something that would add to their sorrow, their tragedy?" Irene kept this secret for over fifty years.

Irene and all twelve of the Jewish people she was hiding survived the war. Irene ended up in a displacement camp and then came to the United States where she married a United Nations official. William Opdyke bragged about his wife's courage at a Rotary Club, where Irene later gave a speech. A local rabbi heard her talk and contacted Yad Vashem, a Holocaust museum in Jerusalem. The people from the museum were able to track down some of the twelve people Irene saved, including the baby that was conceived, and arranged for them to meet.

The man who was that baby conceived at the villa, Roman Haller, said of Irene: "She was and is like a second mother. Without her, I would not be alive." Mr. Haller also noted: "I don't think that there were a lot of people who would risk their own lives for other people. To me, Irene is really an angel."

Irene was honored by Israel as a "Righteous Gentile" and has planted a tree along Yad Vashem's Avenue of the Righteous. "Sometimes it was dangerous, but I wanted to help," said Irene. "I did not think about it. I did not plan it. You did what you did and you did not have time to think. I was young. I had to trust in God. I believe in God and believe no one has a right to kill or murder."

When asked where her courage came from, Irene said: "Courage is a whisper from above. If you think only with your head and not with your heart, the head will tell you, 'Oh, that's danger, don't do this.' So you have to involve your heart."

## Applying the LISTEN Process

Direct the students to their casebook, or photocopy and distribute the LISTEN process handout on page 209 for use with the students.

# Resources for Courage Case 2

## Staring Down AIDS

### Concept Focus: Initiative, Facing Fears

Throughout the discussion of the case, bring up the following points and have the students apply and reflect on them:
- Courage means being so devoted to good that fear does not keep us from doing what is right.
- We gain the strength to claim our fears when we see ourselves in relationship with those who support our efforts and even with those who oppose us.
- Strategies for taming our fears include seeking alternatives, being resourceful, planning ahead, challenging the self, and trying a different perspective.

### *Catechism* Connections

Read the following passages in the *Catechism,* and ask the students to explain how the faith statements can be applied to this case:
- Freedom comes from doing what is good and right. (no. 1733)
- Human virtues guide our conduct. (no. 1804)
- Fortitude is the moral virtue that enables us to conquer fear, even the fear of death. (no. 1808)
- We accept the grace to pursue the virtues through prayer, sacraments, and the life of the church. (no. 1811)

### Scripture Connections

*The Catholic Youth Bible* includes articles on courage:
- "Taking On Goliath" (see 1 Samuel, chapter 17)
- "What Makes a Hero?" (see 1 Macc 9.19–22)
- "Courage" (see Psalm 31)
- "Facing Fear" (see Jer 37.11–21)
- "A Courageous Stance" (see Acts 14.1–7)
- "Homosexuality and AIDS" (see Rom 1.18–32)

### Course Connections

This case can be used with the course *Growing in Christian Morality* with the chapter on courage:
- what we are afraid of (pp. 140–147)
- strategies for taming our fears (p. 148)

## Research for Courage Case 2: Staring Down AIDS

Henry Nichols dealt with two critical medical conditions throughout his life—hemophilia and AIDS. You can pursue further research on these topics by searching Web sites provided by the National Hemophilia Foundation, AEGIS (an AIDS information site), or by logging on to our Faith Community Builders Web site, *www.smp.org/hs,* and searching the links and resources provided there.

## Follow-up for Courage Case 2: Staring Down AIDS

Henry Nichols died on 8 May 2000, at age 26, from injuries that he sustained in a car crash the month before.

# The LISTEN Process Applied

Use the sample questions below to help the students work through the application of the LISTEN process for this case. You may wish to suggest questions for the students or focus on one particular section of the process.

## Look for the Facts

1. What critical decision did Henry face once he found out that he had AIDS?
2. What role did time play in Henry's situation?
3. What facts would you want to know about your medical conditions if you were Henry?

## Imagine Possibilities

1. If you discovered that you had AIDS and had only a short time to live, what possible options would you see for yourself?
2. What would be the short- and long-term consequences of choosing to go public with a disease such as AIDS? (You may wish to use the consequence tree handout on page 208 for this activity.)

## Seek Insight Beyond Your Own

1. How would the Beatitudes provide guidance in this situation?
2. What advice would you expect to hear from your family and friends if you chose to go public with your illness?
3. What types of agencies or support groups are available in your area for people with AIDS? How might one of these agencies be a support for you?

## Turn Inward

1. What would you hope to accomplish by going public with your story? What would motivate you to do so?
2. What would you most want from the decision you would make?
3. Discuss the following quote from Henry and tell whether this would match your attitude:

    To tell you the truth, I don't lose sleep over AIDS anymore. If anything, I lose sleep over not getting my homework done. There are worse fears than the fear of dying, you know.

4. Put yourself in the situation of having Henry as your best friend. How would you respond to him telling you he has AIDS?

## Expect God's Help

1. Compose a prayer for someone suffering from AIDS.
2. Read Psalm 31. How might that Scripture reading comfort and challenge you if you were making the decision presented in this case?

## Name Your Decision

1. What decision would you make if you were Henry? Why?
2. What core values are being upheld in living out that decision?

### Final Questions and Thoughts on Courage Case 2:
### Staring Down AIDS

1. Whom do you most identify with in this case? Why?
2. Put yourself in the position of Henry's parents. What would you advise him to do?
3. What lingering questions or thoughts do you have after reflecting on this case?

# Courage Case 2

## Staring Down AIDS

When Henry Nichols was told that he was HIV positive and could develop AIDS, he was not all that shaken because he had lived with another life-threatening illness, hemophilia, all his life. Henry had contracted HIV at age thirteen after receiving a blood transfusion as treatment for hemophilia. Four years later he developed full-blown AIDS.

When Henry's dad told him that the doctors estimated that he would probably live only a few years more, Henry said, "That sucks," and started to cry. Henry's dad said that overall his son dealt with the situation with a tremendous amount of courage, but "like anyone else who has to face the possibility of death, he gets scared and angry at times."

When Henry was first diagnosed, the family kept his disease private because they wanted him to be treated normally and not as a sick person. But it was only a matter of weeks before Henry decided to tell people. Henry was in Boy Scouts and wanted to work toward the honor of Eagle Scout. He thought that talking openly about his illness could be good for him and the community. "As an Eagle Scout I have to be a leader. I can't be fearful of how the world might react to my having AIDS," he said.

His first step was to tell his eight closest friends. His best friend, Chris Van Cour, said: "At first we were shocked to hear it. A lot of us cried, but then we realized we've got to be strong for him."

The next day Henry and his family held a press conference in Cooperstown, New York. "I felt like a huge load had been removed from my back," said Henry. "For years I had lived with this secret and the fear of how terribly people could react."

Henry started giving presentations about AIDS to high school and college students across the state of New York. Henry has told his audiences that ignorance is dangerous: "No one should have to suffer from AIDS or the ignorance of friends, family, and the community. My Eagle project is not necessarily about AIDS. It's about compassion, understanding, and love."

## Applying the LISTEN Process

Direct the students to their casebook, or photocopy and distribute the LISTEN process handout on page 209 for use with the students.

# Resources for Courage Case 3

**Saving Her Children**

## Concept Focus: Split-Second Decisions, Facing Death

Throughout the discussion of the case, bring up the following points and
have the students apply and reflect on them:
- *Courage* is the ability to do good in the face of harm or the threat of
  injury, whether physical or psychological.
- Situations calling for courage involve naming, claiming, and taming our
  fears. Typical fears include rejection, failure, loss, humiliation, and
  injury—even death.

## Scripture Connections

Have the students read John 15:12–14 (no greater love than to lay down
one's life for a friend) and reflect on its connection to the case.

## Course Connections

This case can be used with the course *Growing in Christian Morality* with
the chapter on courage:
- what we are afraid of (pp. 140–147)

# The LISTEN Process Applied

Use the sample questions below to help the students work through the application of the LISTEN process for this case. You may wish to suggest questions for the students or focus on one particular section of the process.

## Look for the Facts

1. What is the critical decision Leslie had to make in this situation?
2. What specific information would you seek in assessing a dangerous situation like Leslie's?
3. How important is time in a situation like this?

## Imagine Possibilities

1. What were Leslie's options for dealing with the fire?
2. What would be the short- and long-term consequences of choosing to go back into the house? (You may wish to use the consequence tree handout on page 208 for this activity.)

## Seek Insight Beyond Your Own

1. Read John 15:12–14. Based on your reading and understanding of this passage, what would you think Jesus would do in Leslie's situation? Why?
2. What would your family and friends say to you after you called for help?

## Turn Inward

1. What strong feelings could you imagine having in this situation?
2. How would your experiences possibly affect the decision to go into the house after the children?
3. How would you respond to a life-death situation with little time to process all the options for action?

## Expect God's Help

1. Compose a prayer that you would pray to help you make a decision in this situation.
2. Read Psalm 91. How might that Scripture reading comfort and challenge you if you were making decisions like the ones in this case?

## Name Your Decision

1. What decision would you make in Leslie's situation?
2. What core values are being upheld in living out that decision?

## Final Questions and Thoughts on Courage Case 3:
## Saving Her Children

1. Whom do you most identify with in this case? Why?
2. How would the fact that you had another child still living affect your decision to go inside the house after the others?
3. How can one be a hero in personal daily interactions?
4. Do you think you will ever be in a life-death situation?
5. What lingering questions or thoughts do you have after reflecting on this case?

# Courage Case 3

## Saving Her Children

Leslie Hibbs was a young mother of four children, living in Louisville, Kentucky. One early morning in late May, a fire broke out in the house. Leslie ran outside, screaming for help, and then raced back in to save her three youngest children. Her oldest daughter was staying at a friend's house.

The fire department was called and arrived five minutes later. Leslie Hibbs was found unconscious on a bedroom floor, holding her eight-month-old daughter, Faith. The three children died after reaching the hospital. Leslie never regained consciousness, and the doctors told her family that she was brain dead. She died when the respirator was removed a few days later.

"I want her to be remembered as being brave, strong, having the courage of a thousand men to run back into that fire knowing she was out and she could have stayed out," said Leslie's brother, Phillip. "But she knew her kids were there, and it makes me proud."

Leslie's oldest daughter, Melba, asked that Mariah Carey's song "Hero" be played at her funeral. The minister at her church commented, "She put the care and welfare of these precious children above all other things, and she went back in."

## Applying the LISTEN Process

Direct the students to their casebook, or photocopy and distribute the LISTEN process handout on page 209 for use with the students.

# WHOLENESS

Toward Strength, Beauty, and Happiness

# Theme Section Resources

## Discussion-Starter: Give me a LISTEN!

*Vary the way you discuss and process the cases in your classroom. Try this idea during one of the cases in this section.*

Divide the class into six groups and assign each group one letter (*L, I, S, T, E,* or *N*) that corresponds with a step in the LISTEN decision-making process. After students have read a case, either as homework or together in class, have each group focus their discussion on their assigned LISTEN step. Allow ten minutes for the groups to meet and make notes. Then invite each small group to present a summary of their discussion to the class. After each group presents, ask the whole class if there is anything that could be added or that needs further explanation. You may also vary this with the groups by asking them to sing their summaries, prepare transparencies for the overhead or create a computer-based presentation, or dramatize the struggle in the decision.

## Faith Application

After discussing the cases in this theme section, ask the students to consider an action step that would move what they have learned out into the world. Consider these possibilities:

- designing a program to take into elementary school classes that focuses on positive body images
- learning how the media and advertising companies help to form unhealthy body images in young people
- incorporating the theme of wholeness into a prayer service for the school or in another school-wide format
- making personal contracts regarding dependencies—for example, abstaining from watching television for a week

## Opening Prayer

*(See handout on next page.)*

# A Prayer For Wholeness

*Leader:* Holy God, you call us to wholeness.

*All:* Balance.

*Reader 1:* May we strive to keep our priorities straight and live healthy lives.

*All:* Harmony.

*Reader 2:* May we see the interconnectedness of our lives.

*Leader:* Creator God, you call us to holiness.

*All:* Prayer.

*Reader 3:* May we spend time each day centering in the quiet spot of our hearts where you dwell.

*All:* Worship.

*Reader 4:* May we recognize the importance of praying with a community of faith.

*Leader:* Loving God, you call us to relationship.

*All:* Friends.

*Reader 5:* May we affirm and challenge those close to us.

*All:* Family.

*Reader 6:* May we grow to appreciate how our parents and extended family root us.

*Leader:* God of peace, you call us to walk with you.

*All:* May we look for healthy and wholesome ways to authentically be ourselves. In this way we give you all we have—our very lives. May we work to bring glory to your name. We ask this in Jesus' name. Amen.

# Resources for Wholeness Case 1

## Living High

### Concept Focus: Being "Hooked" and Unfree

Throughout the discussion of the case, bring up the following points and have the students apply and reflect on them:

- We are on a journey to *wholeness*—the integrating of all the parts of the self to create a dynamic and harmonious order. When we are whole, we can think "with our heads within our hearts," integrating our thinking with our feelings.
- When we are whole, we can pay attention to the long view and not only to short-term impulses. *Self-restraint* is the channeling and controlling of our drives and impulses into creating wholeness and integrity.
- When we are whole, we are not in the grip of or hooked by *dependencies*. Dependencies on alcohol, other drugs, or casual sex are examples of unfree behaviors that are obstacles to deeper joys and lasting happiness.
- People can become dependent on many things, psychologically as well as physically. Freeing ourselves entails struggle, but freedom is attainable through concentrated effort, community support, and God's grace.

### *Catechism* Connections

Read the following passages in the *Catechism,* and ask the students to explain how the faith statements can be applied to this case:

- We are to avoid excess of every kind. (no. 2290)
- Drug use causes great harm to human health and life. (no. 2291)

### Scripture Connections

*The Catholic Youth Bible* includes an article on addiction:

- "Addictive Behavior" (see 1 Cor 10.6–14)

### Course Connections

This case can be used with the course *Growing in Christian Morality* with the chapter on wholeness:

- short-term versus long-term pleasures (p. 159)
- addiction taking away freedom (pp. 163–166)

## Research for Wholeness Case 1: Living High

The drug crystal methamphetamine (meth) works like other stimulants by sending a message to brain cells to produce excess dopamine, a feel-good chemical that is critical to normal brain functioning. Hours later these cells begin to turn off, slowing the flow of dopamine. Other stimulants allow brain cells to capture and repackage the extra dopamine prompted by the drug, but meth does not, and this makes it especially dangerous because brain cells respond by releasing an enzyme to lessen the dopamine. With repeated meth use, these enzymes eventually kill off the dopamine-creating cells, chemically changing the way the brain works.

You can pursue further research on this topic by logging on to our Faith Community Builders Web site, *www.smp.org/bs,* and searching the links and resources provided there.

# The LISTEN Process Applied

Use the sample questions below to help the students work through the application of the LISTEN process for this case. You may wish to suggest questions for the students or focus on one particular section of the process.

## Look for the Facts

1. What is the key decision Renee needs to make in this case?
2. How do Renee's decisions about drugs change—and stay the same—as she gets older?
3. What type of drug is crystal methamphetamine, and how does it affect the body?

## Imagine Possibilities

1. What are all the possible choices that Renee could make in her situation?
2. What are the short- and long-term consequences of her potential decisions? (You may wish to use the consequence tree handout on page 208 for this activity.)

## Seek Insight Beyond Your Own

1. Whom would you turn to for advice if you were Renee?
2. What advice would your friends give you about using drugs?
3. What legal issues need to be considered when making a decision like Renee's?
4. How could the fifth commandment, "Do not kill," guide someone considering drug use?

## Turn Inward

1. What are your feelings about this situation?
2. What could possibly be the motivation for someone choosing to use harder drugs?
3. What impact would Renee's previous drug experiences have on her deciding whether to use crystal methamphetamine?

### Expect God's Help

1. Compose a prayer for someone struggling with drug addiction or tempted to use hard drugs.
2. Read 1 Corinthians 10:6–14. How might that Scripture reading comfort and challenge you if you were making decisions like the ones in this case?

### Name Your Decision

1. If you were in Renee's situation, what would you decide?
2. What core values are being upheld in living out that decision?

### Final Questions and Thoughts on Wholeness Case 1: Living High

1. Whom do you most identify with in this case? Why?
2. What types of changes face junior high students? Do you understand how Renee felt?
3. How does a twelve-step program like Alcoholics Anonymous help someone with an addiction?
4. What lingering questions or thoughts do you have after reflecting on this case?

# Wholeness Case 1

## Living High

Before seventh grade, Renee enjoyed her life, getting good grades and feeling happy. But then her life started to fall apart. Her parents were going through a divorce. She began to feel different from other kids.

Renee began making new friends with the "stoners" who wore Grateful Dead T-shirts and did some drugs and drinking. "Alcohol made me forget that I hated myself," explained Renee. "It made life seem more tolerable." And when she tried pot for the first time, she found that she liked it better than drinking.

One night during high school, Renee was hanging out with Melissa and her boyfriend, Joe, who were older and into crystal methamphetamine. Feeling pressured by her new friends and thinking that trying it once couldn't hurt her, Renee decided to snort the powder. After she inhaled the powder, she felt its effects. "My eyes were open wider, my heart was beating faster, and I felt an intense rush of happiness," said Renee. "Suddenly everything in my world seemed right."

Renee's spiral into addiction began that night. When she told her other friends that she tried meth, they pleaded with her not to do it again. One friend told her that she had heard that you could get addicted after only a few times. Renee did not see what the big deal was because she had only used it once.

During the next year, Renee found that alcohol and pot were not enough, so she began hanging out with people who used crystal meth. She pulled away from school friends and spent all her money on drugs. When Maggie, a good friend, confronted Renee about her drug use and weight loss, Renee begged Maggie not to call her mom and promised that she would stop. That promise did not last. Renee's life revolved around meth.

Renee's friends went to her mother and told her about the drug use. Renee entered treatment and went through a terrible withdrawal. She then started a twelve-step program and stuck with it. She avoided the kids who did drugs and hung out with the friends who had turned her in to her mom. "Being clean in high school was a challenge," said Renee. "But I did it, and graduated on time with the rest of my class."

In her third year of sobriety, Renee reflected on the wonderful relationships she had with her family, friends, and boyfriend: "Three years ago, I thought my life would be over if I stopped getting high. I was wrong. Getting sober has given me my life back."

## Applying the LISTEN Process

Direct the students to their casebook, or photocopy and distribute the blank LISTEN process handout on page 209 for use with the students.

# Resources for Wholeness Case 2

**Teen Parents**

## Concept Focus: Responsibility, Chastity

Throughout the discussion of the case, bring up the following points and have the students apply and reflect on them:

- We are on a journey to *wholeness*—the integrating of all the parts of the self to create a dynamic and harmonious order. When we are whole, we can think "with our heads within our hearts," integrating our thinking with our feelings.
- When we are whole, we can pay attention to the long view and not just to short-term impulses. *Self-restraint* is the channeling and controlling of our drives and impulses into creating wholeness and integrity.
- When we are whole, we are not in the grip of or hooked by *dependencies*. Dependencies on alcohol, other drugs, or casual sex are examples of unfree behaviors that are obstacles to deeper joys and lasting happiness.
- The Christian understanding is that sex is not intended for short-term pleasure or to express a passing attraction but is a part of a committed, lasting relationship that is based on love and is open to new life. The church's rationale for promoting self-restraint from sexual intercourse until marriage is grounded in concern for the well-being of the persons involved as well as for the life that might come from their union.

## *Catechism* Connections

Read the following passages in the *Catechism,* and ask the students to explain how the faith statements can be applied to this case:

- Chastity involves the integrity of the person. (no. 2337)
- Chastity requires mastery of our passions and impulses. (no. 2339)
- Sexual union between unmarried people is gravely contrary to dignity and sexuality. (no. 2353)

## Scripture Connections

*The Catholic Youth Bible* includes articles that relate to this case:

- "A Fresh Start" (see Psalm 51)
- "Irresponsible Children" (see Ezek 23.1–21)
- "Living Well" (see 1 Cor 6.12–20)

## Course Connections

This case can be used with the course *Growing in Christian Morality* with the chapter on wholeness:

- restraint and passion (pp. 171–172)
- the call to chastity (pp. 173–177)

## Research for Wholeness Case 2: Teen Parents

Teenagers who marry before age eighteen face a much higher rate of divorce statistically. You can pursue further research on this topic by logging on to our Faith Community Builders Web site, *www.smp.org/hs,* and searching the links and resources provided there.

# The LISTEN Process Applied

Use the sample questions below to help the students work through the application of the LISTEN process for this case. You may wish to suggest questions for the students or focus on one particular section of the process.

## Look for the Facts

1. What type of relationship do Wendy and Jason have?
2. What critical decision does Wendy face?
3. What facts would you want to know in order to make a good decision involving teen pregnancy?

## Imagine Possibilities

1. Once discovering the pregnancy, what choices does Wendy have? Jason? (You may wish to use the consequence tree handout on page 208 for this activity.)
2. What are the short- and long-term consequences for each potential decision?

## Seek Insight Beyond Your Own

1. What advice would your friends give you about pregnancy? How would this advice be affected by the gender of your friends?
2. If you were to talk to your parents, what would they say about a pregnancy?
3. Does your school handbook have guidelines regarding teen pregnancy? What are they? How could they help you make a good decision?
4. What guidance could the church offer in this situation?

## Turn Inward

1. What are your feelings about this case?
2. How would your experiences affect your attitudes, thoughts, and decision involving teen pregnancy? Give examples of this.
3. How would your conscience guide you in making this decision?
4. After you make the decision, what would you want to feel?
5. What is the relationship between Wendy and Jason like? How would that relationship affect the decision about the pregnancy?

## Expect God's Help

1. Compose a prayer for students who are facing a teen pregnancy.
2. Read Psalm 31:1–5. How might that Scripture reading comfort and challenge you if you were making decisions like the ones in this case?

## Name Your Decision

1. What decision would you make if you were Wendy? Jason?
2. What core values are being upheld in living out that decision?

### Final Questions and Thoughts on Wholeness Case 2: Teen Parents

1. Whom do you most identify with in this case?
2. If you were the administrator of a school or the teacher in a classroom, how would you go about talking to students about teen pregnancy and parenthood?
3. Are you aware of any programs in your area that provide counseling and support to teen parents?
4. What lingering questions or thoughts do you have after reflecting on this case?

## Teen Parents

Wendy Besinaiz met Jason Sanden at school. They were part of the same peer group and Wendy really liked him. Jason was known for being a tough kid who fought with other guys, was disrespectful with teachers, and was quite popular. "Yeah, he was the most popular kid in school," said Wendy. "All the girls wanted to go out with him."

Wendy's friends told her that Jason would never go out with her, but Jason did ask her out. Wendy would sneak out of her house and stay the night at Jason's. Wendy thought Jason's mom was "cool," and they grew quite close. However, Wendy's own mother acknowledged that Wendy was out of her control.

Wendy was a virgin and Jason respected that. "He didn't pressure me at all," she said. "He never did anything I didn't want to do."

One day when Wendy went over to Jason's house to watch a video, there was a rose on his bed. "It was so romantic. I was scared. I was terrified. We just laid there. I didn't think it was going to happen," explained Wendy. "But we started kissing and stuff. And it just happened."

Wendy and Jason became sexually active, and Wendy eventually found herself pregnant. At first she was in denial, hiding her growing stomach from her mother. Her mother had told Wendy that she would kick her out of the house if she got pregnant. Knowing this, Wendy ran away and began living with Jason and his mother. Jason's mom thought Wendy was good for Jason; she "softened" him and made him more interested in school.

There was never any doubt about having the baby, according to Wendy: "I always told myself if I got pregnant, I would keep the baby no matter if I went on welfare or whatever. Abortion I couldn't do because that's a part of me, and I couldn't. Adoption I couldn't do either. No doubt about it, it was going to be mine."

When the baby was born, Wendy and Jason named her Veronica. Jason was in the delivery room, along with his mom. Jason's mom cared for the baby while Wendy went to school on a reduced schedule. Jason took a job on a loading dock and has stopped attending night school. Wendy has said that she enjoys being a mom, although Veronica's "incessant crying" gets on her nerves.

## Applying the LISTEN Process

Direct the students to their casebook, or photocopy and distribute the LISTEN process handout on page 209 for use with the students.

# Resources for Wholeness Case 3

## Dying to Be Whole

### Concept Focus: Wholeness (Not Perfection), Peace with Self

Throughout the discussion of the case, bring up the following points and have the students apply and reflect on them:
- We are on a journey to *wholeness*—the integrating of all the parts of the self to create a dynamic and harmonious order. When we are whole, we can think "with our heads within our hearts," integrating our thinking with our feelings.
- Becoming whole means becoming unique, not becoming perfect. We become whole as we invest in our personal gifts and goals.
- Inner disunity may be reflected in how we treat ourselves physically. An eating disorder can be a sign of low self-esteem.

### Catechism Connections

Consider looking up the following passage in the Catechism, and ask the students to explain how the faith statement can be applied to this case:
- Morality rejects the idolization of physical perfection. (nos. 2289–2290)

### Scripture Connections

*The Catholic Youth Bible* includes an article on eating disorders:
- "It's What's Inside That Counts" (see 2 Cor 5.1–5)

### Course Connections

This case can be used with the course *Growing in Christian Morality* with the chapter on wholeness:
- unity, order, and direction (p. 167)
- in touch with one's needs (p. 167)
- body image (pp. 168, 170)

### Research for Wholeness Case 3: Dying to Be Whole

You can pursue further research on this topic by logging on to our Faith Community Builders Web site, *www.smp.org/hs,* and searching the links and resources provided there.

## Follow-up for Wholeness Case 3: Dying to Be Whole

Three years after Heidi died, her mother, Patricia Harrington, filed a lawsuit against the Boston Ballet and artistic director Anna-Marie Holmes. She claimed that the company was "recklessly and grossly negligent" in asking her daughter to lose weight. She also claimed that the company should have known that Heidi was suffering from anorexia nervosa.

The autopsy performed on Heidi's body found the cause of death to be an irregular heartbeat. The lawsuit claims that the eating disorder was the cause of the heart problem.

# The LISTEN Process Applied

Use the sample questions below to help the students work through the application of the LISTEN process for this case. You may wish to suggest questions for the students or focus on one particular section of the process.

## Look for the Facts

1. What is the key decision for Heidi in this case?
2. How do comments from other people affect Heidi's image of her body and herself? What possible motives did these people have for their comments?
3. What do you know about anorexia nervosa?

## Imagine Possibilities

1. What are all the possible ways Heidi could have dealt with the pressure to be thin? (You may wish to use the consequence tree handout on page 208 for this activity.)
2. How could the ballet company have handled their comments differently?

## Seek Insight Beyond Your Own

1. Whom would you turn to for advice if you were Heidi?
2. What advice would your family and friends give you if they thought you were not eating or not healthy?
3. What counseling services could be available in the community?

## Turn Inward

1. What are your feelings about this situation? How would you deal with the pressure to be thin and perfect?
2. How much control do you think Heidi likely had over her eating disorder before she went on the trip to Disneyland with her brother and mother?
3. If you were Heidi, how important would the external comments and advice be from the art directors of the ballet company?
4. Do you have an intuitive understanding of this case? Explain.

## Expect God's Help

1. Compose a prayer for someone dealing with an eating disorder or someone who struggles with body image.
2. Read 2 Corinthians 5:1–5. How might that Scripture reading comfort and challenge you if you were making decisions like the ones in this case?

## Name Your Decision

1. If you were in Heidi's situation, how would you handle the suggestion to lose weight?
2. What core values are being upheld in living out that decision?

### Final Questions and Thoughts on Wholeness Case 3: Dying to Be Whole

1. Whom do you most identify with in this case? Why?
2. Did Heidi's mother have a substantial claim in filing the lawsuit against the Boston Ballet and its artistic director? Explain.
3. How widespread do you believe eating disorders are in your school?
4. How important is body image to teenagers? Where does this image come from? What do you believe can be done about it?
5. Do you have any lingering thoughts or questions after reflecting on this case?

# Wholeness Case 3

## Dying to Be Whole

Heidi Guenther was born in San Diego, California, as the oldest of three children. Her physical gifts were striking even as an infant. "She was always into things," her father, Richard, remembered, "climbing on things." She walked at eight months and at age six she blossomed in dance classes. "She loved dancing," her dad said.

Heidi's mother encouraged and supported her aspiration to become a professional dancer. At age eleven Heidi was accepted into a summer program at the Houston Ballet School. She moved on to the San Francisco Ballet School from 1987–1994, where she was a scholarship student. Her friend and fellow dancer, Melanie Brown, said: "She was so focused and driven to succeed. All she wanted was to be a ballerina."

When Heidi's body started to undergo puberty, she became uncomfortable with her developing breasts. "She didn't want them," explains her sister, Kirsten. That was also the year the ballet company told Heidi to lose weight. "It was just devastating to hear," her mother said. After Heidi lost a few pounds, she still went out to eat with her friends. She did not seem obsessed with losing weight.

Several years later, Heidi was an apprentice with the Boston Ballet. Anna-Marie Holmes, the artistic director, suggested to Heidi that if she lost five pounds off her 115-pound frame, she would have a better chance of joining the main company. According to Holmes, "You see a girl on stage, her butt going up and down, it's not attractive." Holmes said that diversity in body types existed in the Boston Company. "Our company is not a company of sticks . . . but you have to have some aesthetic value. People are paying for tickets to see you." The director of the ballet agreed, saying that Heidi "had gotten just a little pudgy at that point."

Heidi did drop the weight, and a year later she was promoted to the main dancing corps of the Boston Ballet. Months later at her evaluation, Heidi's dancing was praised but she was also told to be careful about getting too thin and to be sure to eat well. Routine physicals later that year with the company's doctor and nutritionist noted no "serious problems" with Heidi. The artistic director noted that "she was thin, but not thin to the point of dying."

When summer came, Heidi went home. Her mother recalled that "she was thin, too thin, and I said that to her." Heidi's response was that she would gain a few pounds. Her sister said that even a size one was baggy on her. In addition to this, Heidi had started smoking. Her spirits were good, and she ate small portions at meals. No one ever caught her throwing up. "If I had thought there was an eating disorder, I would have acted on it," said her mother.

On the way to an annual visit to Disneyland with her mother and brother, Heidi was having a good time. After stopping at a convenience store, Heidi suddenly fell backward in the minivan. "No gasp, no cry, no nothing," said her mother. "When I opened the door and she fell out, her eyes were fixed, her lips were blue." Heidi's mother screamed for her to wake up, but Heidi never did. Her heart had stopped. Less than an hour later, she was pronounced dead at a local hospital. At the time of her death, Heidi was 5'3" and weighed ninety-three pounds.

## Applying the LISTEN Process

Direct the students to their casebook, or photocopy and distribute the LISTEN process handout on page 209 for use with the students.

# Resources for Wholeness Case 4

## Bulking Up

### Concept Focus: Wholeness (Not Perfection)

Throughout the discussion of the case, bring up the following points and have the students apply and reflect upon them:

- We are on a journey to *wholeness*—the integrating of all the parts of the self to create a dynamic and harmonious order. When we are whole, we can think "with our heads within our hearts," integrating our thinking with our feelings.
- Becoming whole means becoming unique, not becoming perfect. We become whole as we invest in our personal gifts and goals.
- Inner disunity may be reflected in how we treat ourselves physically. Steroid use can be a sign of low self-esteem.

### *Catechism* Connections

Read the following passage in the *Catechism*, and ask the students to explain how the faith statements can be applied to this case:

- Drug use causes great harm to human health and life. (no. 2291)

### Scripture Connections

*The Catholic Youth Bible* includes an article that relates to steroid use:

- "It's What's Inside That Counts" (see 2 Cor 5.1–5)

### Course Connections

This case can be used with the course *Growing in Christian Morality* with the chapter on wholeness:

- unity, order, and direction (p. 167)
- in touch with one's needs (p. 167)
- body image (pp. 168, 170)

### Research for Wholeness Case 4: Bulking Up

- You can pursue further research on this topic by searching Web sites provided by the National Institute on Drug Abuse or by logging on to our Faith Community Builders Web site, *www.smp.org/hs*, and searching the links and resources provided there.

## Follow-up for Wholeness Case 4: Bulking Up

The students may benefit from knowing more of the effects of steroid abuse. In males the abuse can shrink the testicles and cause irreversible baldness, impotence, and breast enlargement.

In females steroid abuse can deepen the voice and cause facial hair to grow. Bone growth can be stunted in both sexes, and major organs, such as the heart, liver, and kidneys, can be permanently damaged.

# The LISTEN Process Applied

Use the sample questions below to help the students work through the application of the LISTEN process for this case. You may wish to suggest questions for the students or focus on one particular section of the process.

## Look for the Facts

1. What is the key decision Bill must make in this case?
2. What facts would you want to know in order to make a good decision?
3. In what ways do boys feel pressure about their body image?

## Imagine Possibilities

1. What are all the possible ways Bill could deal with his feelings of inadequacy?
2. What are the short- and long-term consequences for those potential decisions? (You may wish to use the consequence tree handout on page 208 for this activity.)

## Seek Insight Beyond Your Own

1. Whom would you turn to for advice if you were Bill?
2. What advice would your friends give you about using steroids?
3. What would the coaches and personal trainers you know say about steroid abuse?
4. Is there any legal issue to consider in deciding whether or not to use steroids?

## Turn Inward

1. What are your feelings about this situation?
2. What could possibly be the motivation for someone choosing to use steroids? Do you understand this motivation?
3. How would your conscience help guide you in deciding whether to use steroids?

## Expect God's Help

1. Compose a prayer for someone struggling with body image or steroid use.
2. Read 1 Corinthians 3:16–20. How might that Scripture reading comfort and challenge you if you were making decisions like the ones in this case?

## Name Your Decision

1. If you were in Bill's situation, what would you decide?
2. What core values are being upheld in living out that decision?

## Final Questions and Thoughts on Wholeness Case 4: Bulking Up

1. Whom do you most identify with in this case? Why?
2. How does the image of the perfect body differ for boys and girls?
3. Do you believe steroid abuse is a problem among people you know?
4. According to a study in the book *The Adonis Complex: The Secret Crisis of Male Body Obsession* (The Free Press, 2000), American men would like to add twenty-eight pounds of muscle to their bodies, and more than half of the teenage boys surveyed chose a body image impossible to achieve without the use of steroids. Dr. David Rosen, chief of teenage and young adult health at the University of Michigan has said: "When anabolic steroids first came out, they were used to enhance sports performance. Over the past ten years or so, almost half the boys who use steroids don't use them for sports, but to look better." Do you agree with these thoughts? Explain fully.
5. What lingering questions or thoughts do you have after reflecting on this case?

### Bulking Up

Just as Barbie has shaped the body image for girls, the evolution of action dolls marketed for boys may be doing the same. Dr. Harrison Pope Jr., a psychiatrist in Belmont, Massachusetts, has studied how each new version of the G.I. Joe action figure has become more muscular and sharply defined. Other action dolls, such as Batman, have seen the same phenomenon. This could be planting a seed in boys' minds that in order to look good they must have bulging biceps and a small waist—a body that is unrealistic and unattainable without going to unhealthy extremes. Bob Goldman, a Chicago osteopath, has noted that boys learn that the ideal man looks like Mr. Universe. "Watch Saturday morning television, and you'll see all these huge, abnormally muscled beings on cartoons and kids' programming."

Bill was seventeen years old and a junior at a high school in New England before he started taking steroids. He thought he was a "wallflower" with only a couple of friends. After taking sixteen cycles of steroids over the course of two years, Bill became more confident and had many friends.

One day Bill's parents found a needle that he forgot to throw away. They helped him make some immediate changes in his life and helped him stop using steroids. Bill recalled, "I had to switch gyms because they [his friends] were all teasing me about shrinking up and pressuring me to use the stuff."

His friends bet that he would go back to steroids. Bill countered honestly: "Right now, the only way I know I'll stay off steroids is if I can find a guarantee that I'll reach 220 pounds without them. No, make that 230."

## Applying the LISTEN Process

Direct the students to their casebook, or photocopy and distribute the LISTEN process handout on page 209 for use with the students.

# HONESTY
Creating Trust

### Discussion-Starter: WORD-O-GRAM

*Vary the way you discuss and process the cases in your classroom. Try this idea during one of the cases in this section.*

Have the students write the letters in the word *honesty* down the left margin of a piece of paper. Before or after the discussion of one of the cases, challenge the students to think of a word, phrase, or sentence that begins with each letter *(H, O, N, E, S, T, and Y)* and relates to the case. After giving the students some time in class or assigning this as homework, use these acronyms as discussion-starters.

## Faith Application

After discussing the cases in this theme section, ask the students to consider an action step that would move what they have learned out into the world. Consider these possibilities:
- organizing a school-wide campaign to get rid of cheating, with a slogan such as, "Cheating cheats you!"
- focusing school-wide prayer on the theme of honesty for one week

## Opening Prayer

*(See handout on next page.)*

# A Prayer for Honesty

*Leader:* Loving God, you are a God of truth. You draw us to you and invite us to live our lives honestly and authentically. We ask you to hear our petitions this day.

*Reader 1:* For the times we are tempted to lie,

*All:* give us the courage to tell the truth.

*Reader 2:* When we are faced with a situation where the easy way out would be to omit certain facts,

*All:* let us see the big picture and keep it whole.

*Reader 1:* When we become tangled in our rationalizations,

*All:* let us see that honesty is the way out of the web of deceit.

*Reader 2:* For the times when the little white lies cover up the truth,

*All:* let us embrace integrity as a guiding virtue.

*Reader 1:* When we are faced with moments of truth telling,

*All:* let us speak with kindness and love.

*Reader 2:* For the times when we are caught in a lie of our own,

*All:* let us be called to truth and to accept responsibility.

*Leader:* Jesus, you spoke the truth with love. You challenged and comforted with that truth. Show us how to live this way. Fill us with a love of truth that will bring us to fullness of life.

*All:* Amen.

# Resources for Honesty Case 1

**Driving Honesty**

## Concept Focus: Conscience, Healthy Guilt

Throughout the discussion of the case, bring up the following points and have the students apply and reflect on them:

- *Honesty*, the willingness to seek and uphold the truth, enables us to live in the real world. Truth frees us. As the adage says, when we tell the truth, we don't have to remember what we said. Lies shackle us to false realities and faked memories.
- Honesty keeps society healthy, builds trust in personal relationships, and rewards us by building personal integrity and wholeness.
- Honest people are skilled at listening to what is going on inside them. They stay in tune with who they really are, what they really think, how they really feel.
- Honesty often has costs. But by creating a world of trust, honesty ultimately buys more than it costs.

## *Catechism* Connections

Read the following passages in the *Catechism,* and ask the students to explain how the faith statements can be applied to this case:

- Deliberate retention of lost goods is against the seventh commandment. (no. 2409)
- Truthfulness is a virtue in human action and speech. (no. 2468)
- Honor gives witness to human dignity. (no. 2479)
- Lying is destructive to society and relationships. (no. 2486)
- The duty of reparation exists when there is an offense against justice or truth. (no. 2487)

## Scripture Connections

*The Catholic Youth Bible* includes an article on honesty:
- "Nothing But the Truth" (see Prov 10.18–21)

## Course Connections

This case can be used with the course *Growing in Christian Morality:*
- healthy guilt (p. 86)
- the benefits of being honest (pp. 180–181)

# The LISTEN Process Applied

Use the questions below to help the students work through the application of the LISTEN process for this case. You may wish to suggest questions for the students or focus on one particular section of the process.

## Look for the Facts

1. If you were in this situation on the highway, what facts would you want to know?
2. Who were all the people and parties involved in this situation?

## Imagine Possibilities

1. What are all the possible choices that could be made in this situation? (You may wish to use the consequence tree handout on page 208 for this activity.)
2. What would the short- and long-term consequences be if Melvin kept the money?

## Seek Insight Beyond Your Own

1. If you had your best friend in the car with you and the money bags were thrown open in front of you, what advice would you expect to hear from your friend?
2. What would your parents advise you to do in this situation? What do you think *they* would do? Ask them.
3. How could the seventh and tenth commandments provide guidance in this case? Would taking the money really be stealing?
4. Read Matthew 22:21. How might this Scripture reading give you input on how Jesus would approach this situation?

## Turn Inward

1. What would motivate you to grab as much money as you could?
2. What would motivate you to drive by without stopping?
3. How would your conscience play a role in making a decision?

## Expect God's Help

1. What would you pray for to help you in making the right decision?
2. Read Proverbs 21:2–3. How might that Scripture reading comfort and challenge you if you were making a decision like the one in this case?

## Name Your Decision

1. What decision would you make in Melvin's situation?
2. What core values are being upheld in living out that decision?

### Final Questions and Thoughts on Honesty Case 1: Driving Honesty

1. Share with the students this additional piece of information from the case: At the time of the accident, a man who worked in urban planning stopped his car on an overpass and took pictures of the motorists grabbing the money. He later turned the film over to the police.
2. Would this additional piece of information influence your decision to keep or return the money? Why or why not?
3. What lingering questions or thoughts do you have after reflecting on this case?

## Driving Honesty

Early one morning in October, Ohio Bell telephone repairman Melvin
Kiser was driving in downtown Columbus. On the highway in front of
him was an armored car. "Then I see its doors open and a bag fall out,"
remembered Melvin. "The car ahead of me hits it, and the bag busts open.
It was like a heavy snowfall." What came out of the bags was approxi-
mately two million dollars in unmarked ten, twenty, fifty, and hundred dol-
lar bills! The truck did not brake or stop.

Many motorists stopped their cars and started to stuff their clothing
and bags with the money. One person yelled, "Money! Money! Grab some
while you can!" Another exclaimed, "It's a gift from heaven!" Melvin
grabbed a torn bag of money and headed back home, shaking. When he
started driving, he began thinking about a new tractor for his new forty-
acre farm.

About twenty minutes later, the armored truck returned, along with
the police. About $500,000 was recovered at the scene, but over $1.5 million remained with the motorists who stopped their vehicles.

Melvin called his fiancée, Vickie, and told her about his good fortune.
He was laughing, and she thought the whole thing was a joke. But he
told her: "I'm serious. I was thinking about keeping it, but I'm going to
give it back to the police."

Melvin did go to the local police precinct to turn in the money. There
was an incredulous look on the officers' faces when he did that. The
Metropolitan Armored Car Company paid a 10 percent reward for any
cash returned, so Melvin earned $5,767.

Melvin said he was raised to be an honest person and that his mother
was proud of him. His dad, on the other hand, told his son: "I thought I
raised you better than that! I would have headed south so fast I'd have
burned out two trucks." Melvin remained steadfast in his decision, saying,
"I couldn't have lived with myself if I'd kept it."

## Applying the LISTEN Process

Direct the students to their casebook, or photocopy and distribute the LIS-
TEN process handout on page 209 for use with the students.

# Resources for Honesty Case 2

## An Epidemic of Cheating

## Concept Focus: Rationalization

Throughout the discussion of the case, bring up the following points and have the students apply and reflect on them:

- *Honesty*—the willingness to seek and uphold the truth—enables us to live in the real world. Truth frees us. As the adage says, when we tell the truth, we don't have to remember what we said. Lies shackle us to false realities and faked memories.
- Honesty keeps society healthy, builds trust in personal relationships, and rewards us by building personal integrity and wholeness.
- Honest people are skilled at listening to what is going on inside them. They stay in tune with who they really are, what they really think, and how they really feel.
- *Self-deception* means fooling ourselves about our reasons for doing something. Self-deception often goes hand-in-hand with the deception of others. *Rationalizations* are examples of self-deception.

## *Catechism* Connections

Read the following passages in the *Catechism,* and ask the students to explain how the faith statements can be applied to this case:

- Truthfulness is a virtue in human action and speech. (no. 2468)
- Lying is destructive to society and relationships. (no. 2486)

## Scripture Connections

*The Catholic Youth Bible* includes an article on honesty:

- "Nothing But the Truth" (see Prov 10.18–21)

## Course Connections

This case can be used with the course *Growing in Christian Morality* with the chapter on honesty:

- self-deception (p. 185)
- accepting the possibility of failure (pp. 189–190)
- losing power and control (p. 190)

## Research for Honesty Case 2: An Epidemic of Cheating

You can pursue further research on this topic by logging on to our Faith Community Builders Web site, *www.smp.org/hs,* and searching the links and resources provided there.

# The LISTEN Process Applied

Use the sample questions below to help the students work through the application of the LISTEN process for this case. You may wish to suggest questions for the students or focus on one particular section of the process.

## Look for the Facts

1. What type of school stress did Leigh face?
2. What types of cheating went on in the school?
3. What is the critical decision Leigh faced?
4. Leigh saw herself as treated unfairly by teachers. Was she?
5. How is cheating a form of lying? stealing?

## Imagine Possibilities

1. Besides cheating in some form, what other options would Leigh have for preparing for tests? (You may wish to use the consequence tree handout on page 208 for this activity.)
2. What are the short- and long-term consequences for cheating?

## Seek Insight Beyond Your Own

1. What advice would your friends give you about cheating?
2. If you were to talk to your parents, what would they say about cheating?
3. Does your school handbook have guidelines regarding cheating? What are they? How could they help you make a good decision?
4. Which commandment could provide guidance in choosing whether or not to cheat?

## Turn Inward

1. What are your feelings about the current epidemic of cheating?
2. What would tempt you to cheat on a test? Why?
3. How would your conscience guide you in making that decision?
4. After you make the decision, how would you want to feel?

## Expect God's Help

1. Compose a prayer for students who are stressed out and tempted to cheat on a test.
2. Read Proverbs 13:5. How might that Scripture reading comfort and challenge you if you were making decisions like the ones in this case?

## Name Your Decision

1. What decision would you make if you were Leigh?
2. What core values are being upheld in living out that decision?

### Final Questions and Thoughts on Honesty Case 2:
### An Epidemic of Cheating

1. Would you categorize cheating as an "epidemic" in your school?
2. A survey from the Joseph and Edna Josephson Institute of Ethics found that 70 percent of high school students admitted to cheating on a test at least once in the past year. Does this number seem high or low to you? Why?
3. If you were the administrator of a school or a teacher in a classroom, how would you go about changing attitudes and practices of cheating students?
4. What lingering questions or thoughts do you have after reflecting on this case?

# Honesty Case 2

### An Epidemic of Cheating

It never fails that many teachers decide to test on the same day. "There's no one who could remember that much info," says Leigh Milender.

Faced with the mounting pressure, Leigh routinely cheats on chemistry tests by copying formulas into her graphing calculator.

Leigh believes that most teachers are naive about this technology, and that they "haven't caught up with the times."

Other students in her school cheat regularly. She says that she has seen kids "write answers on the inside of a shoe, roll a cheat sheet inside a ballpoint pen, copy term papers from the Internet."

There are different types of cheating, according to Leigh and her peers. "Copying term papers [from the Internet] is the dishonest kind of cheating," she says. "And people who cheat off other people are dishonest cheats. They're hurting themselves. I'll admit I've cheated, but not off anyone else. I just think it's fine if you're taking a test and a couple of formulas might help you out. But that's the farthest I've gone."

According to Leigh, cheating will continue "until testing becomes fair, because every teacher thinks she's the only one in the world to assign a test that Friday."

## Applying the LISTEN Process

Direct the students to their casebook, or photocopy and distribute the LISTEN process handout on page 209 for use with the students.

# Resources for Honesty Case 3

## Little Big Lies

### Concept Focus: False Excuses, Responsibility

Throughout the discussion of the case, bring up the following points and have the students apply and reflect on them:

- Honesty keeps society healthy, builds trust in personal relationships, and rewards us by building personal integrity and wholeness.
- White lies are supposedly innocent untruths that do not hurt anyone. That's usually an excuse for our avoiding truth-telling.
- Honesty often costs us. But by creating a world of trust, honesty ultimately buys more than it costs.
- "Love and truth will meet" (Psalm 85:11, NAB). We are called to speak our truth—what we see or feel—without judging the other person. This leaves the door open to our hearing what the other person may see or feel. The truth may be bigger than we first thought.

## *Catechism* Connections

Read the following passages in the *Catechism*, and ask the students to explain how the faith statements can be applied to this case:

- Truthfulness is a virtue in human action and speech. (no. 2468)
- Friendship and the desire to be of service does not justify white lies. (no. 2480)
- Lying is destructive to society and relationships. (no. 2486)

## Scripture Connections

*The Catholic Youth Bible* includes an article on honesty:

- "Nothing But the Truth" (see Prov 10.18–21)

## Course Connections

This case can be used with the course *Growing in Christian Morality* with the chapter on honesty:

- self-deception (p. 185)
- accepting the possibility of failure (pp. 189–190)
- problems with white lies (pp. 191–191)

# The LISTEN Process Applied

Use the sample questions below to help the students work through the application of the LISTEN process for this case. You may wish to suggest questions for the students or focus on one particular section of the process.

## Look for the Facts

1. What were the facts of this situation?
2. Who was involved in the decision?
3. How did Gail's job play a role in this decision?
4. How was the element of time a crucial point in the case?

## Imagine Possibilities

1. What options did Gail have after she discovered the news about the World Trade Center? (You may wish to use the consequence tree handout on page 208 for this activity.)
2. What choices could Gail have made before leaving on the ski trip that could be more preventative as opposed to reactive?
3. What potential short- and long-term consequences did Gail face by choosing to lie to her boss?

## Seek Insight Beyond Your Own

1. What advice would your friends give you about lying to the boss about where you had been over the weekend?
2. What commandment has the underlying value of honesty? How might that guide your decision?

## Turn Inward

1. What are your feelings about different types of lying: white lies, half-truths, lies of omission?
2. What would lead you to make up a story to an authority figure like a boss, teacher, or parent?
3. How would your conscience guide you in making that decision?
4. What would you want to feel after making the decision? How could that guide you?

## Expect God's Help

1. Compose a prayer asking for wisdom and courage for Gail.
2. Read Proverbs 21:6. How might that Scripture reading comfort and challenge you if you were making a decision like the one in this case?

## Name Your Decision

1. What decision would you make if you were Gail?
2. What core values are being upheld in living out that decision?

### Final Questions and Thoughts on Honesty Case 3: Little Big Lies

1. If you were Gail's boss, how would you handle her lying? Why? What consequences would you expect to give her?
2. Do you believe that some lies come from low self-esteem?
3. What types of false excuses do you hear at school?
4. A survey from the Joseph and Edna Josephson Institute of Ethics found that 92 percent of high school students admitted to lying to their parents and 78 percent admitted lying to a teacher. Do these statistics surprise you? Do they ring true? Why or why not?
5. What lingering questions or thoughts do you have after reflecting on this case?

# Honesty Case 3

## Little Big Lies

Gail and her boyfriend left one weekend for a skiing trip in Vermont. Gail was a twenty-two-year-old assistant producer at a local television station in the state of New York and new to the job. Part of her work meant being available at all times because major news stories could break at any time. "There's an iron-clad rule," Gail recalled, "that everyone in the news department must check in regularly when they're out of the office."

That Friday was the 1993 bombing of the World Trade Center. So during the weekend, a big story in the history of New York City occurred. Gail was enjoying her weekend and did not call in even once. The farmhouse that she and her boyfriend were staying in did not have a phone.

Gail did not find out about the bombing until Sunday night. On Monday she went to her boss's office and told him that she had been in the hospital with a concussion and wasn't able to phone the office.

Her boss said, "Why didn't you go the whole way and tell me you had brain surgery?" He told her that he could forgive her for not staying in touch with the office, but the lie was a big mistake. Gail's boss told her that every job in television has hundreds of applicants.

Gail did not get fired but said she has learned her lesson—always tell the truth.

## Applying the LISTEN Process

Direct the students to their casebook, or photocopy and distribute the LISTEN process handout on page 209 for use with the students.

# RESPECT FOR PEOPLE

## Looking Again

# Theme Section Resources

## Discussion-Starter: Symbol Papers

*Vary the way you discuss and process the cases in your classroom. Try this idea during one of the cases in this section.*

Using only clippings, pictures, collages, or symbols, ask the students to illustrate the key themes and lessons from one of the cases. The students can share these in small or large groups by simply holding them up for others to see. After a period of time where the students look carefully at one another's work, allow them to ask questions and discuss the impact of certain pictures or illustrations. Use these comments as a springboard for class discussion.

## Faith Application

After discussing the cases in this theme section, ask the students to consider an action step that would move what they have learned out into the world. Consider these possibilities:

- Pair up with another school in an area that has a different make-up than your school. Work to build relationships with each other and build some bridges!
- Design an "Empathy Appeal" that educates classmates and the community about the virtue of empathy. Consider collecting "pledges" and designing fun activities to raise the awareness of the need for empathy in our world.
- Invite someone to speak to your classes or the whole school community about racial discrimination.

## Opening Prayer

*(See handout on next page.)*

# A Prayer for Respect for People

*Leader:* Every person counts in the Christian vision! Loving God, let us see with your eyes.

*Reader 1:* In Jesus' day the lepers were separated from the rest of society. No one dared talk to them, much less touch them.

*All:* May we reach out to those who feel that they are on the outside of our groups.

*Reader 2:* Christ ate with sinners, women, and even tax collectors. He accepted their hospitality and enjoyed their company.

*All:* May we work to be more inclusive with all people.

*Reader 3:* Jesus cured the blind man, and the blind man saw for the very first time.

*All:* May we open our eyes and see the beauty of each individual whom we know and meet.

*Leader:* Empathy is the ability to understand another's feelings, thoughts, experiences, and point of view.

*Reader 1:* Let us use our imagination to feel another's pain.

*Reader 2:* Let us learn the stories of our brothers and sisters who have experienced the pain of discrimination.

*Reader 3:* Let us become aware of the ignorance within so that we can seek wisdom and understanding.

*Reader 4:* Let us enter into relationships committed to the Golden Rule.

*All:* Do to others whatever you would have them do to you.

*Reader 1:* Accept me.

*Reader 2:* Listen to me.

*Reader 3:* Laugh with me.

*Reader 4:* Talk to me.

*Reader 5:* Include me.

*Reader 6:* Sit with me.

*Reader 7:* Invite me.

*Reader 8:* Get to know me.

*Leader:* God, you know us. You sent us Jesus Christ to show us how to live, how to treat others. Open our ears to the stories of our brothers and sisters. Open our minds and hearts to see what Jesus calls us to live out each day. We ask you to be with us now and always. Amen.

**Handout F**

## Abusive Relationships

### Concept Focus: Unhealthy Relationships, Emotional Abuse

Throughout the discussion of the case, bring up the following points and have the students apply and reflect on them:

- Respect for people is grounded in the Golden Rule, and it builds upon *empathy*—our ability to understand another's feelings, thoughts, and experiences.
- No one wants to be used or manipulated for someone else's purposes. Christians are challenged to value other people as worthy in themselves, apart from what they can do for us. The tendency to use and manipulate others can develop into a way of life that destroys the capacity for genuine friendship.
- Physical, emotional, and psychological violence are serious forms of disrespect for people. Psychological abuse or manipulation can be just as destructive as physical abuse because it can be more easily hidden.

### *Catechism* Connections

Read the following passages from the *Catechism,* and ask the students to explain how the faith statements can be applied to this case:

- Do to others whatever you would have them do to you. (no. 1970)
- Respect the dignity of the person. (no. 1929)

### Scripture Connections

*The Catholic Youth Bible* includes articles on abuse that are relevant to this case:

- "Love and Jealousy" (see Gen 16.1–16)
- "Hagar's Rescue" (see Gen 21.8–21)

### Course Connections

This case can be used with the course *Growing in Christian Morality* with the chapter on respect for people:

- respect for people (pp. 197–199)
- to be treated with care, not violence (pp. 201–203)

## Research for People Case 1: Abusive Relationships

Physical, emotional, and psychological abuse is a serious problem in teen relationships. You can pursue further research on this topic by logging on to our Faith Community Builders Web site, *www.smp.org/hs,* and searching the links and resources provided there.

## Additional Activities for People Case 1: Abusive Relationships

This story deals with emotional abuse. Consider asking the students to explore the issues of domestic violence and physical abuse. Ask the students to examine how abuse can escalate in a relationship.

# The LISTEN Process Applied

Use the sample questions below to help the students work through the application of the LISTEN process for this case. You may wish to suggest questions for the students or focus on one particular section of the process.

## Look for the Facts

1. What were the warning signs that something was not right in Kelly and Matt's relationship?
2. What was the critical decision that Kelly needed to make?
3. What other information would you want to know before making a decision like Kelly's?

## Imagine Possibilities

1. What options did Kelly have for dealing with her relationship with Matt? (You may wish to use the consequence tree handout on page 208 for this activity.)
2. What short- and long-term consequences would be part of each option?

## Seek Insight Beyond Your Own

1. If you were in an unhealthy relationship, to whom would you turn for advice?
2. What would you expect that your family and friends would say to you about an unhealthy relationship?
3. Is the way that Matt treated Kelly sinful? Why?
4. What commandments or beatitudes could be used for guidance in this situation?
5. Is emotional abuse illegal? Should it be?

## Turn Inward

1. Do you think that you would seek out help if you were in an unhealthy relationship? Why or why not?
2. What needs did Kelly have that she thought Matt filled?
3. What would your conscience tell you to do if you were in Kelly's position?
4. How can you tell if you are being manipulated in a relationship? Explain.
5. What do you think was going on in Matt's mind as he abused Kelly?

## Expect God's Help

1. Compose a prayer especially for someone in an abusive relationship.
2. Read Psalm 140. How might that Scripture reading comfort and challenge you if you were making decisions like Kelly's?

## Name Your Decision

1. What decision would you make if you were in a relationship like Kelly and Matt's?
2. What core values are being upheld in living out that decision?

### Final Questions and Thoughts on People Case 1:
### Abusive Relationships

1. Whom do you most identify with in this case? Why?
2. Do you believe that anyone can get caught up in an unhealthy relationship? Why or why not?
3. Many times people in unhealthy relationships describe themselves as feeling "trapped." Why is this?
4. What lingering questions or thoughts do you have after reflecting on this case?

# People Case 1

## Abusive Relationships

Kelly met Matt shortly after her parents finalized their divorce. Matt was a really passionate person. When others told Kelly that he was manipulative, she did not listen to them.

Over time Matt began to make negative comments about Kelly's friends. He would tell her that she needed new clothes and makeup. He would tell her that she was stupid and immature and not learning anything in school. Sex became a manipulative activity as well.

"He wasn't physically beating or battering me at all, but he was just digging away at me emotionally, like relentlessly insulting me, embarrassing me," said Kelly. "I was totally controlled by him. So it was more subtle than physical abuse, but it was just as damaging."

Kelly began to believe many of Matt's comments and looked up to him. She desperately wanted his approval and began to feel trapped. "I just didn't mentally know how to get myself out of it," Kelly reflected. "I couldn't deal with the pain of having to get myself out of it."

When Kelly confronted Matt about how he treated her, he turned on her, calling her crazy and saying that everything was her fault. He even locked her in a room for a night and would not let her come out. Still Kelly thought it was her fault and that she needed to talk with him.

When Kelly found out that Matt had stolen money from her family, he tried to manipulate the situation by telling her that she had said it was okay to take the money and spend it. This is when Kelly realized that the relationship was out of control. "Why would I tell him that he could take my family's money and spend it? And I realized this is what he was doing all along," Kelly exclaimed. "He was trying to make me believe that I was crazy."

Kelly had an incredible amount of sadness bottled inside her and acknowledged that the relationship was making her feel like she was dying inside. After the breakup she felt ashamed to talk to her friends because she didn't think they would understand the strong and out-of-control feelings that she had.

Kelly believes that Matt took away her trust of people and much of her self-confidence. But she knows too that she has gained a knowledge and an understanding that she won't let it happen to her again.

## Applying the LISTEN Process

Direct the students to their casebook, or photocopy and distribute the LISTEN process on page 209 for use with the students.

# Resources for People Case 2

## Concept Focus: Discrimination, Prejudice, Stereotypes

Throughout the discussion of the case, bring up the following point and have the students apply and reflect on it:

- We all have the right to be accepted as individuals, not put down or labeled because we belong to a certain group. A *stereotype* is an oversimplified picture of members of a group based on assumptions that may have little or no basis in fact. Stereotyping reduces us to objects or tools for others' use.

## *Catechism* Connections

Read the following passages from the *Catechism*, and ask the students to explain how the faith statements can be applied to this case:

- Respect the human person. (no. 1931)
- "The equality of men rests essentially on their dignity as persons and the rights that flow from it." (no. 1935)

## Scripture Connections

*The Catholic Youth Bible* includes articles on prejudice and stereotypes:

- "A Prayer Against Prejudice" (see Joshua, chapter 2)
- "Discrimination in Jesus' Time" (see Luke 10.25–37)
- "Seeing with God's Eyes" (see John, chapter 9)
- "Stretch Me, Lord" (see Acts 11.1–18)

## Course Connections

This case can be used with the course *Growing in Christian Morality* with the chapter on respect for people:

- respect for people (pp. 197–199)
- stereotypes and prejudice (pp. 208–209)
- melting the prejudice barrier (pp. 210–212)

## Research for People Case 2: Who Belongs?

Students who are unfamiliar with sororities and fraternities may benefit from some background and history on Greek organizations. A good resource is the *Encarta Encyclopedia* online article that details the history, background, and structure of both sororities and fraternities. You can pursue further research on this topic by logging on to our Faith Community Builders Web site, *www.smp.org/bs,* and searching the links and resources provided there.

## Follow-up for People Case 2: Who Belongs?

University of Georgia officials have decided to bring an educational sanction against the Alpha Gamma Delta sorority. This resolution calls for the sorority to undergo sensitivity training and take on a leadership role in promoting racial diversity on campus. The university agreed to lift the suspension that kept the sorority from participating in the social functions of the school and Greek system.

# The LISTEN Process Applied

Use the sample questions below to help the students work through the application of the LISTEN process for this case. You may wish to suggest questions for the students or focus on one particular section of the process.

## Look for the Facts

1. What are the key facts in this situation?
2. Why do you think this situation occurred?
3. What was the primary decision Allison faced in this situation?
4. What additional information would you want in order to make a decision in this situation?

## Imagine Possibilities

1. What are all the options Allison had for dealing with the comments she heard from her sorority sisters? (You may wish to use the consequence tree handout on page 208 for this activity.)
2. What consequences, both short- and long-term, did each option entail? Explain each fully.
3. What was the most loving response Allison could have made? Why?

## Seek Insight Beyond Your Own

1. If you heard racist comments made, to whom would you turn for advice? What would they say to you?
2. How do you believe Jesus would handle this situation? Can you think of any Scripture passages in which Christ confronted discrimination? Explain them.
3. Was there a legal issue in this case?

## Turn Inward

1. How would your feelings come into play in this situation? What experiences in your life might influence you?
2. What would motivate you to go public with the comments you heard? What would motivate you to stay silent?
3. How conflicted would you feel in this situation? Why?
4. Why do you believe the girls in the sorority would make comments about the potential member's race? What do you believe is going on inside those girls?

## Expect God's Help

1. Read the prayers found in *The Catholic Youth Bible* on pages 217, 1260, and 1298. How might those prayers comfort and challenge you if you were making a decision like Allison's?
2. What prayer would you offer for the students who made the racist remarks?

## Name Your Decision

1. What decision would you make? Why?
2. What core values are being upheld in living out that decision?
3. Would you leave the university as Allison did after you made your decision? Why or why not?

## Final Questions and Thoughts on People Case 2: Who Belongs?

1. Whom do you most identify with in this case? Why?
2. If another sorority accepted a student just because she was African American, would that be respectful?
3. The story does not follow the student who was not allowed in the sorority. If you knew who she was, would you talk with her after the incident? Why or why not? What would you say?
4. Racism still touches the lives of many people today. Do you think that this will get better or worse in your lifetime? Explain.
5. What lingering questions or thoughts do you have after reflecting on this case?

# People Case 2

## Who Belongs?

Allison Davis decided that she wanted to be a student at the University of Georgia when she was a junior in high school. She knew that she wanted to be involved in campus life and believed that membership in a sorority would be a good way to accomplish this goal.

In the fall of 1999, Allison decided that she would try to join Alpha Gamma Delta because she thought it was a sorority that "valued diverse backgrounds, ideas, and perspectives." Before she could become a member, she would have to be evaluated by the current sorority members and other potential candidates to see if she would "fit in" with the organization. Allison passed the evaluation and joined the sorority that year.

The following fall the sorority chapter came together to vote on whether "low-scoring recruits" would be accepted into Alpha Gamma Delta. One of these girls was an African American student whose individual scores were either very high or extremely low. Allison heard the sorority sisters who gave her the low scores make comments that were blatantly racist. One allegedly said, "If we had a black girl in our sorority, none of the fraternities would want to do anything with us." The majority of the chapter voted the African American student out.

Allison was very upset and decided to take the issue to the executive council of the sorority and then to the administration of the university. While the issue was being looked into, Allison was treated poorly by sorority members who made insulting faces and insensitive comments to her. She claimed that they accused her of overreacting "to an issue that just wasn't that important."

Allison decided to withdraw from the University of Georgia and return home. The issue has been likened to a wake-up call as the university decided to investigate the sorority and require diversity training for the University of Georgia's twenty-seven fraternities and sororities.

## Applying the LISTEN Process

Direct the students to their casebook, or photocopy and distribute the LISTEN process handout on page 209 for use with the students.

# Resources for People Case 3

### Concept Focus: Emotional Abuse, Hatred

Throughout the discussion of the case, bring up the following points and have the students apply and reflect on them:
- Respect for people is grounded in the Golden Rule, and it builds upon *empathy,* the ability to understand another's feelings, thoughts, and experiences from that person's point of view.
- People want to be valued, not used, by others; treated with care, not violence; and accepted as individuals, not stereotypes. *Stereotyping* reduces us to objects or tools for others' use.
- *Prejudice* continues in society through ethnic and racial jokes and slurs, indifference or disrespect toward members of other groups. Most prejudice is rooted in fear and ignorance, and in insecurity about oneself.

### *Catechism* Connections

Read the following passages in the *Catechism,* and ask the students to explain how the faith statements can be applied to this case:
- Looking upon your neighbor as "another self." (no. 1931)
- Discrimination is incompatible with God's design. (no. 1935)

### Scripture Connection

*The Catholic Youth Bible* includes an article on anti-Semitism and the Nazis' plan for genocide:
- "Body Count" (see Esth 3.1–7)

### Course Connections

This case can be used with the course *Growing in Christian Morality* with the chapter on respect for people:
- respect for people (pp. 197–199)
- stereotypes and prejudice (pp. 208–209)
- melting the prejudice barrier (pp. 210–212)

### Research for People Case 3: Intimidation

You can pursue further research on this topic by logging on to our Faith Community Builders Web site, *www.smp.org/hs,* and searching the links and resources provided there.

# The LISTEN Process Applied

Use the sample questions below to help the students work through the application of the LISTEN process for this case. You may wish to suggest questions for the students or focus on one particular section of the process.

## Look for the Facts

1. What were the ways that Alon was being harassed? Why was this happening?
2. What critical decision did Alon face in this situation?

## Imagine Possibilities

1. What are all the ways that Alon could have dealt with the harassment? (You may wish to use the consequence tree handout on page 208 for this activity.)
2. What potential outcomes could have come from each of these options?

## Seek Insight Beyond Your Own

1. What advice would you seek from your family if you were in Alon's situation?
2. What legal issues were involved in the harassment Alon experienced?
3. What advice would your friends give you if you were Alon?
4. What would Jesus do?

## Turn Inward

1. How would you feel if you were persecuted for your family background and religion? Why?
2. What motives could a person possibly have for harassing someone?
3. What would you need most from the decision you would make?

## Expect God's Help

1. Compose a prayer that you would pray if you were being harassed and persecuted unfairly.
2. Read Psalm 17. How might that Scripture reading comfort and challenge you if you were in Alon's situation?

## Name Your Decision

1. How would you choose to deal with this situation?
2. What core values are being upheld in living out that decision?

## Final Questions and Thoughts on People Case 3: Intimidation

1. Whom do you most identify with in this case? Why?
2. What is at the root of hatred and persecution?
3. Have you heard of any incidents of anti-Semitism where you live?
4. React to Alon's statement, "A lot of people were against the Nazi regime, but no one did anything, and then it was too late."
5. What lingering questions or thoughts do you have after reflecting on this case?

# People Case 3

## Intimidation

Alon Aloni grew up in a Jewish family, always being comfortable with his religion. He had never experienced any anti-Semitism or violence directly until his sophomore year in high school. In his sophomore English class, a boy wearing a ring with a swastika on it sat near him. When Alon asked him if he knew what the swastika meant, the boy acknowledged that he did and was aware that it offended people.

From that point on, the boy started to harass Alon by tapping the ring on his desk, or clicking his heels together and yelling out, "Heil Hitler" or "White Power." Other Jewish students at the school didn't want to get involved in the situation, and Alon found himself alone in his concerns: "He kept doing these things in the hall," explained Alon. "He'd do it in front of a lot of people and no one would get involved."

Alon went to the vice principal and filed a complaint. After the vice principal talked to the boy, the boy's father called Alon's mother and said that he had taken the ring away from his son.

Nevertheless, the harassment continued, and Alon's grades suffered. Alon became very frightened and did not want to go to the school bathroom by himself. One day in class, the English teacher showed a video about World War II. "Every time it mentioned Hitler, or the gas chambers, and all the people who passed away," explained Alon, "he would laugh or tap on the desk with his finger."

Once Alon overheard the boy in the hall, kicking the walls saying: "This is how I'm going to kill the . . . Jew, Alon, this is how I'm going to kill him. I'm going to kick him in the head." After Alon reported this incident to the vice principal, he decided to file a police report. The boy was suspended for two days and eventually was transferred to another school. But the next semester, he came back. When Alon saw him in the hall, staring at him, he realized he had to leave the school. He had heard rumors that the boy had a gun at school.

When the story came out, other students shared similar stories that had happened to them. Alon also found that many students sympathized with him but wouldn't jump on the bandwagon to do anything about it at the time. Alon reflected: "And that's what happened in Germany. A lot of people were against the Nazi regime, but no one did anything, and then it was too late. That can happen anywhere. And with an attitude like 'I don't want to stand up for what's right,' that's gonna happen."

## Applying the LISTEN Process

Direct the students to their casebook, or photocopy and distribute the LISTEN process handout on page 209 for use with the students.

# COMPASSION

## Solidarity with Those Who Suffer

# Theme Section Resources

## Discussion-Starter: Compassion Poems

*Vary the way you discuss and process the cases in your classroom. Try this idea during one of the cases in this section.*

Poetry can be an effective way of starting discussion because it can engage both mind and heart. In preparation for these cases, ask the students to write a short poem with the theme of compassion. You can offer various poem prompts or forms, such as haiku, where the students write three lines, the first line with five syllables, the second line with seven syllables, and the third line with five syllables. Or the students can write an acronym poem, taking the letters of the word *compassion* and writing words or phrases that begin with each of the letters.

Before discussing the case, ask the students to share their poetry in small groups. Each small group can select the poem that is most touching, powerful, and effective, and then share it with the large group. After each reading, discuss how the poem speaks of compassion for and solidarity with those who suffer.

## Faith Application

After discussing the cases in this theme, ask the students to consider an action step that would move what they have learned out into the world. Consider these possibilities:

- Set up a family service opportunity with Habitat for Humanity or Christmas in April. Recruit families from your school to participate.
- Sponsor a "Day of Compassion" at your school or in your community.

## Opening Prayer

*(See handout on next page.)*

# A Prayer for Compassion

*Leader:* Let us call to mind the words of the prophet Isaiah.

*All:* Sing for joy, O heavens, and exult, O earth; break forth, O mountains, into singing! For the Lord has comforted his people, and will have compassion on his suffering ones.

*Reader 1:* For the lonely and scared.

*All:* The Lord has comforted his people and will have compassion on his suffering ones.

*Reader 2:* For the rejected and disenfranchised.

*All:* The Lord has comforted his people, and will have compassion on his suffering ones.

*Reader 3:* For those in pain and hurting.

*All:* The Lord has comforted his people, and will have compassion on his suffering ones.

*Reader 4:* For the homeless and poor.

*All:* The Lord has comforted his people, and will have compassion on his suffering ones.

*Reader 5:* For those who are bitter and angry.

*All:* The Lord has comforted his people, and will have compassion on his suffering ones.

*Reader 6:* For those who have lost loved ones.

*All:* The Lord has comforted his people, and will have compassion on his suffering ones.

*Leader:* Sing for joy, O heavens, and exult, O earth; break forth, O mountains, into singing!

*All:* How can we rejoice when there are so many suffering?

*Leader:* You can be the hands of Christ.

*Reader 1:* I can smile at someone who seems lonely.

*All:* How can we rejoice when there are so many suffering?

*Leader:* You can be the hands of Christ.

*Reader 2:* I can include those who may otherwise feel rejected.

*All:* How can we rejoice when there are so many suffering?

*Leader:* You can be the hands of Christ.

*Reader 3:* I can embrace and comfort those who are hurting.

*All:* How can we rejoice when there are so many suffering?

*Leader:* You can be the hands of Christ.

*Reader 4:* I can volunteer at a local community center for homeless and poor people.

*All:* How can we rejoice when there are so many suffering?

*Leader:* You can be the hands of Christ.

*Reader 5:* I can offer a soothing word and peace to those who are bitter.

*All:* How can we rejoice when there are so many suffering?

*Leader:* You can be the hands of Christ.

*Reader 6:* I can comfort the sorrowing by my presence.

*Leader:* How can we rejoice when there are so many suffering?

*All:* The Lord will comfort the people and will have compassion for the suffering ones. We are the body of Christ and need to bring that comfort and compassion to our hurting world. Amen.

# Resources for Compassion Case 1

## Concept Focus: Being Sensitive to the Pain of Others

Throughout the discussion of the case, bring up the following points and have students apply and reflect on them:
- Becoming a compassionate person is a life-long process that involves imitating the example of Jesus, turning our own suffering into opportunities to become more sensitive to others.
- Compassion is a way of seeing ourselves as part of and one with all of humanity—united as the *Mystical Body of Christ.*
- Basic knowledge about a particular disability can serve as preventive medicine against stereotyping and prejudice.

## *Catechism* Connections

Read the following passages in the *Catechism,* and ask the students to explain how the faith statements can be applied to this case:
- Solidarity is a requirement of our faith. (no. 1941)
- Handicapped people should be helped to live a normal life. (no. 2276)

## Scripture Connections

*The Catholic Youth Bible* includes articles that contain meaningful connections to this case:
- "Betrayed!" (see Psalm 55)
- "The Tongue: Friend or Foe?" (see Jas 3.1–12)

## Course Connections

This case can be used with the course *Growing in Christian Morality* with the chapter on compassion:
- definition of compassion (pp. 215–216)

## Research for Compassion Case 1: Getting to Know Angie

You can pursue further research on the topic of cerebral palsy by logging on to our Faith Community Builders Web site, *www.smp.org/bs,* and searching the links and resources provided there.

# The LISTEN Process Applied

Use the sample questions below to help the students work through the application of the LISTEN process for this case. You may wish to suggest questions for the students or focus on one particular section of the process.

## Look for the Facts

1. What is the major decision Angie must make?
2. Why is this situation happening with Angie's peers?
3. What decision faces Angie's peers?

## Imagine Possibilities

1. What options does Angie have for dealing with the teasing from her peers? (You may wish to use the consequence tree handout on page 208 for this activity.)
2. What are the advantages and disadvantages involved with each option?
3. If Angie's peers feel uncomfortable around Angie, how could they deal with that?

## Seek Insight Beyond Your Own

1. What advice would you give Angie if she were a student at your school?
2. What type of advice would your parents give you?

## Turn Inward

1. How do you think you would feel if you were a teen with cerebral palsy?
2. If you were in Angie's position, what would you want most to come from a decision to speak with your peers about your disability?
3. What possible motives could Angie's peers have for making fun of her?

## Expect God's Help

1. Compose a prayer that you would pray if you were Angie.
2. What prayer would you offer for peers who were teasing Angie and calling her names?
3. Read Psalm 25. How might that Scripture reading comfort and challenge you if you were in Angie's situation?

## Name Your Decision

1. Would you decide to talk to your peers about your disability if you were Angie? Why or why not?
2. If you were a classmate of Angie's and felt uncomfortable around her, how would you behave?
3. What core values are being upheld in living out that decision?

## Final Questions and Thoughts on Compassion Case 1: Getting to Know Angie

1. Whom do you most identify with in this case? Why?
2. How can the virtue of compassion be a guiding principle in this case?
3. Sometimes people who suffer a lot become bitter, closed, or hardened. Do you believe Angie is on this road or another path? Explain.
4. What lingering questions or thoughts do you have after reflecting on this case?

# Compassion Case 1

## Getting to Know Angie

Angie was born with cerebral palsy, a condition that affects her coordination and motor skills, but not her mental capabilities. When she started third grade, people started to see her as different. She wasn't able to write her name, so she used a typewriter. She got behind on her assignments in that grade and was held back. Other kids called her stupid, a retard.

Angie said: "It hurt a lot to be teased by people I thought were my friends. People started commenting on my speech, saying I talked really weird." Angie believes that the kids were afraid of her because she was different. She also believes that few people know much about cerebral palsy.

Angie's peers would make fun of her often. Sometimes Angie would keep it inside and not cry out. Other times she yelled back, cried, and ran away. One time when she was in seventh grade, several kids began tormenting her by calling her names and saying that she should be in kindergarten. After leaving the room crying, she talked with a counselor who encouraged her to talk with her peers and explain her condition. When she did, the other students apologized and stopped bothering her.

Angie believes that people make fun of others because they need attention. "They have problems," she said, "so they hurt others to make themselves feel better."

## Applying the LISTEN Process

Direct the students to their casebook, or photocopy and distribute the LISTEN process handout on page 209 for use with the students.

# Resources for Compassion Case 2

## A Change of Heart

### Concept Focus: Forgiveness, Compassion

Throughout the discussion of the case, bring up the following points and have the students apply and reflect on them:

- *Compassion* is our ability to be conscious of and moved by others' suffering and our desire to alleviate their suffering.
- Becoming a compassionate person is a life-long process that involves our imitating the example of Jesus—turning our own suffering into opportunities to become more sensitive to others, and actively seeking opportunities for compassion through service.
- *Forgiveness* is the decision to let go of resentment, which can hurt us more than those it is directed at. Christians are called to do the hard work of forgiveness, to forgive "seventy-seven times" (Matthew 18:22).

## *Catechism* Connections

Read the following passages in the *Catechism,* and ask the students to explain how the faith statements can be applied to this case:

- Jesus invites us to share in his ministry. (no. 1506)
- Solidarity is a requirement of our faith. (no. 1941)
- Execution of offenders is rarely if ever necessary to protecting the common good. (nos. 2266–2267)
- Living Jesus' commandment to love one another also means forgiving one another. (no. 2842)
- Forgiveness can be a transforming event that turns injury into compassion. (no. 2843)
- Forgiving our enemies is the way to reconciliation. (no. 2844)

## Scripture Connections

*The Catholic Youth Bible* includes articles that connect to Bud's experiences in this case:

- "Letting Go of the Past" (see Gen 33.1–17)
- "Letting Go of Anger" (see Psalm 103)
- "Christians and Revenge" (see Mt 5.38–48)
- "Forgive Us Our Debts" (see Mt 18.21–35)
- "The Reunion Dinner" (see Lk 7.1–10)

## Course Connections

This case can be used with the course *Growing in Christian Morality* with the chapter on compassion:
- definition of compassion (pp. 215–216)
- relationship between compassion and forgiveness (p. 222)

## Research for Compassion Case 2: A Change of Heart

You can pursue further research on this topic by searching sites on the McVeigh trial or by logging on to our Faith Community Builders Web site, *www.smp.org/hs,* and searching the links and resources provided there.

## Follow-up for Compassion Case 2: A Change of Heart

Timothy McVeigh was put to death by lethal injection on Monday, 11 June 2001, six years after he set the bomb that killed 168 people at the Alfred P. Murrah Federal Building in Oklahoma City. He was the first federal prisoner to be executed in thirty-eight years.

# The LISTEN Process Applied

Use the sample questions below to help the students work through the application of the LISTEN process for this case. You may wish to suggest questions for the students or focus on one particular section of the process.

## Look for the Facts

1. What central decision did Bud face after Julie died in the federal building?
2. What decisions did Bud face as the trials of Timothy McVeigh and Terry Nichols happened?
3. What key decision did Bud face when he visited Bill McVeigh?

## Imagine Possibilities

1. What options did Bud have for dealing with his grief? (You may wish to use the consequence tree handout on page 208 for this activity.)
2. What consequences, both short- and long-term, were involved in each option? Explain each fully.
3. What was the most loving response Bud could make? Why?

## Seek Insight Beyond Your Own

1. Whom would you turn to if you were dealing with the tragic death of someone close to you? What do you imagine they would say to you?
2. Would your friends and family support the death penalty for the killers of someone you loved?
3. What are the legal issues involved with the death penalty and life imprisonment?
4. "We pay a high price emotionally when we withhold forgiveness, while doing the hard work of forgiveness helps us to heal." How does this insight fit this case?
5. Read the Beatitudes in Matthew 5:3–12. Do any of those speak to the key issues in this case?

## Turn Inward

1. How would your personal feelings come to play in this situation? What experiences in your own life might influence you?
2. What would motivate you to support the death penalty for the killers?
3. How conflicted would you feel in this situation? Why?
4. What would it take for you to reach a positive outlook on the situation? Why?

## Expect God's Help

1. Read Matthew 5:38–48. How might those words comfort and challenge you if you were in Bud's situation?
2. Compose a prayer that you would use to pray for guidance in this situation.

## Name Your Decision

1. What decision would you make in a situation like this? Why?
2. What core values are being upheld in living out that decision?

### Final Questions and Thoughts on Compassion Case 2:
### A Change of Heart

1. Whom do you most identify with in this case? Why?
2. Would you be able to meet with the family of the person who killed someone you loved? Why or why not?
3. How did Bud truly live out the virtue of compassion, which, at its roots, means, "to suffer with?"
4. What do you believe caused Bud's change of heart?
5. What lingering questions or thoughts do you have after reflecting on this case?

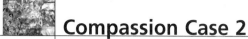

## A Change of Heart

19 April 1995 was a sunny spring day in Oklahoma City. Julie Welch went to work that morning as a Spanish translator and interpreter for the Social Security office in the Alfred P. Murrah Federal Building. At 9:03 a.m. a massive bomb in a rental truck detonated and killed 168 adults and children. Julie Welch was one of them.

Timothy McVeigh and Terry Nichols stood trial and were convicted of committing, at that time, the worst terrorist act on U.S. soil. As the sentencing trials continued over the course of several years, a great momentum arose for these men to receive the death penalty.

During the first four or five weeks of the trial, Julie's dad, Bud Welch, was caught up in that way of thinking as well. "I wanted them fried—I didn't even want trials," he said. "That's normal rage and revenge, a period of temporary insanity." But Bud remembered Julie's adamant opposition to the death penalty. She had said of death penalty supporters, "All they're doing is teaching hate to their children."

Bud began to search his soul and soon realized that the anger was not allowing him to heal. He said: "You can't heal when you carry revenge and hate. The two don't mix. And revenge and hate is exactly why this bomb went off right here." He realized that the death penalty was not the answer. Bud became an advocate against the death penalty and began giving lectures all over the country. When Terry Nichols was given life in prison and people began pushing for another trial and sentence, Bud remained staunchly fixed in his opposition to that. "The man got life. We need to move forward, and some are having a very difficult time doing that. This just prolongs the anger. It just keeps pulling the scab off."

When asked whether he felt any sympathy for Timothy McVeigh, the man who left the truck bomb at the building, Bud realized that forgiveness was essential to moving on with life. "We're supposed to be somewhat spiritual beings, and at some point in time, I'm going to have to forgive him."

On a trip to Buffalo, New York, where he was speaking, Bud decided to visit Bill McVeigh, Timothy's father. When he went to the McVeigh home, Bill's daughter, Jennifer, joined them. Bud happened to see a picture of Timothy in high school, and he kept coming back to it. As tears filled his eyes, Jennifer started crying. Bud said, "Honey, the three of us are in this for the rest of our lives." Bud also promised that he would do everything he could to prevent Timothy's execution. McVeigh ultimately was given the death penalty.

Once back to his hotel, Bud wept for an hour and felt that a large weight was lifted from his shoulders. "I never felt closer to God than I did at that moment." Bud felt compassion towards Bill McVeigh. He said: "In Bill, I had found a bigger victim of the bombing than myself. I get to tell people all about my daughter and how wonderful she was. But Bill, when he meets a stranger, he probably doesn't even tell them he has a son."

Bud realized that forgiveness and compassion was hard work and it took time. "Getting to the point I'm at today is not an event, it's a process," he said.

## Applying the LISTEN Process

Direct the students to their casebook, or photocopy and distribute the LISTEN process handout on page 209 for use with the students.

# Resources for Compassion Case 3

**A Family in Service**

### Concept Focus: Service, Doing for Others

Throughout the discussion of the case, bring up the following points and have the students apply and reflect on them:

- *Compassion* is our ability to be conscious of and moved by others' suffering and our desire to alleviate their suffering.
- *Solidarity* among persons is indicated by a capacity to be together in a supportive but equal way.

### *Catechism* Connections

Read the following passages in the *Catechism,* and ask the students to explain how the faith statements can be applied to this case:

- Jesus Christ invites us to share in his ministry. (no. 1506)
- Solidarity is a requirement of our faith. (no. 1941)
- The works of mercy include sheltering the homeless. (no. 2447)

### Scripture Connections

*The Catholic Youth Bible* includes articles that connect to Nathan's experiences in this case:

- "Called to Follow Jesus" (see Mk 1.16–20)
- "What Do You Want From Me?" (see Mk 12.13–17)
- "Spice Me Up, Lord" (see Lk 14.34–35)
- "Prayer of a Servant Leader" (see Lk 22.24–27)

### Course Connections

This case can be used with the course *Growing in Christian Morality* with the chapter on compassion:

- the works of compassion (p. 216)
- giving and receiving (pp. 217–218)
- opening up one's heart to those in need (pp. 224–225)

### Research for Compassion Case 3: A Family in Service

You can pursue further research on this topic by searching the Web site provided by Christmas in April, *www.rebuildingtogether.org,* or by logging on to our Faith Community Builders Web site, *www.smp.org/hs,* and searching the links and resources provided there.

# The LISTEN Process Applied

Use the sample questions below to help the students work through the application of the LISTEN process for this case. You may wish to suggest questions for the students or focus on one particular section of the process.

## Look for the Facts

1. What central decision did Nathan need to make?
2. What led Nathan's parents to cancel the trip to Disneyland?

## Imagine Possibilities

1. What options did Nathan have? (You may wish to use the consequence tree handout on page 208 for this activity.)
2. What consequences, both short- and long-term, were involved with each option? Explain each fully.
3. What was the most loving response Nathan could have made? Why?

## Seek Insight Beyond Your Own

1. Whom would you turn to for advice on how to handle your parents' decision? What can you imagine they would say to you?
2. Read Luke 16:19–31. How does that Scripture reading give insight into how Jesus would handle this situation? What advice would Jesus give Nathan?

## Turn Inward

1. How would your personal feelings come to play in this situation? What experiences in your own life might influence you?
2. What would motivate you to refuse to go on the family trip or to be negative about the change in plans?
3. How conflicted would you feel in this situation? Why?
4. What would it take for you to reach a positive outlook on the situation? Why?

## Expect God's Help

1. Read Luke 22:24–27. How might those prayers comfort and challenge you if you were in Nathan's situation?
2. Compose a prayer that you would use to pray for guidance in this situation.

## Name Your Decision

1. What decision would you make? Why?
2. What core values are being upheld in living out that decision?

## Final Questions and Thoughts on Compassion Case 3:
## A Family in Service

1. Whom do you most identify with in this case? Why?
2. What do you believe caused Nathan's change of heart?
3. What lingering questions or thoughts do you have after reflecting on this case?

# Compassion Case 3

## A Family in Service

Nathan Smith was looking forward to his family's big trip to Disneyland. In Bountiful, Utah, there are no big amusement parks with exciting rides.

Nathan's dad, Richard Smith, was aware of how comfortably his family lived and wanted to do something to help those who were less fortunate. He and his wife Debbie contacted an organization called Christmas in April, an organization out of Washington, D.C., that works collaboratively with communities across the country to rehabilitate houses of elderly and disabled people. The Smiths decided that the family would work with this group instead of taking a trip to Disneyland.

Nathan and his younger sister, Johnna, were initially very angry about this decision. "I didn't see why I should give up my vacation to work for free helping strangers," said Nathan.

The first part of the trip began with a drive from Utah to Tumacacori, a small community near Nogales, Arizona, about two miles north of the border with Mexico. The people in this village are very poor, and the housing is run down.

The Smith family, along with four other families, was assigned to repair Hermenia Lopez's house. The roof was full of holes, several windows were broken, and one of the doors wouldn't close. "It was an unlivable shack that needed complete rebuilding," recalled Richard. They worked with a team leader and demolished walls, repaired floors, and tarred the roof.

In less than a week, the house was clean and modernized. The eighty-five-year-old owner, Hermenia Lopez, was overwhelmed with joy. "Thank you from the bottom of my heart," she exclaimed in Spanish to the families.

Nathan experienced a change of heart as he worked side by side with his family. He also turned a broken picnic table into one that looked brand new using some sandpaper and paint. "It felt good to be counted on to do something others appreciated," Nathan said.

Nathan's mother, Debbie, was impressed with her son. "The selfish teenager we brought to Tumacacori turned into a skilled and sensitive young man I felt proud of."

During breaks, the families were able to visit a local museum, and they also traveled to Mexico for dinner and cultural workshops. Debbie Smith believes that her whole family learned some life lessons on the trip. "They learned that any life worth living involves giving to others."

## Applying the LISTEN Process

Direct the students to their casebook, or photocopy and distribute the LISTEN process handout on page 209 for use with the students.

# RESPECT FOR CREATION
The Earth As God's

## Discussion-Starter: Hot Chair

*Vary the way you discuss and process the cases in your classroom. Try this idea during one of the cases in this section.*

Set up a chair and a bell or buzzer at the front of the classroom. Put red streamers around the chair or a piece of a paper on it, marking it as the "Hot Chair." Explain to students that this chair is to be used when an individual or a group has a "hot" question that is particularly provocative. That person comes to the chair, rings the bell or buzzer, and, when the class is quiet, shares the hot question with everyone. The previous discussion should stop, and responses to the new question should be shared in small groups or large group. If needed, pass out six hot sticks (red question cards, each attached to a stick) to the students to ensure that questions will keep popping up. You may want to use hot cinnamon candies or other hot candies as an incentive.

## Faith Application

After discussing the cases in this theme, ask the students to consider an action step that would move what they have learned out into the world. Consider these possibilities:

- Organize a community clean-up effort or a school-wide recycling program.
- Publish a simple-living column in your school newspaper.
- Plan an opportunity in your school community or neighborhood to plant trees.

## Opening Prayer

*(See handout on next page.)*

# A Prayer for Creation

*Leader:* Creator God, you have shared with us a great gift—the earth.

*Reader 1:* We praise you for the beauty that surrounds us each day.

*Reader 2:* The sky above us—blue, gray, cloudy, sunny, starry, streaming with streaks of color.

*Reader 3:* The plants and trees, flowers and bushes—brown, green, changing color with each season.

*Reader 4:* The people that we meet and know—their smiles and tears, their laughter and pain.

*Leader:* We know the earth is hurting. God, give us the courage to respond to the needs of creation.

*Reader 1:* Pollution, strip mining, acid rain.

*All:* Heal the earth, God.

*Reader 2:* Litter, urban sprawl, toxic waste.

*All:* Heal the earth, God.

*Reader 3:* Abuse, overload, wastefulness.

*All:* Heal the earth, God.

*Leader:* We hear the earth singing to give praise to God.

*Reader 4:* The sun, the moon, the shining stars!

*Reader 5:* The earth, the waters, the rain, snow, and frost!

*Reader 6:* The mountains, hills, trees, and flowers!

*All:* We praise you, God. May we be a healing presence in our world and take care of all creation! Amen.

# Resources for Creation Case 1

## Caring for the Environment

### Concept Focus: Action Versus Apathy

Throughout the discussion of the case, bring up the following points and have the students apply and reflect on them:

- We respect God's creation when we see all created things—living and nonliving—as good in themselves. *Ecological justice* involves the obligations that we as humans have to the rest of creation.
- We respect creation when we study and support the interconnected and dynamic balance within creation.
- We respect creation when we take care of it as part of our efforts to build the Reign of God. Humans are causing and tolerating widespread environmental damage to the earth and its atmosphere. Specific actions by individuals and groups can reverse and prevent such damage and make a huge impact on the future of the earth.

### *Catechism* Connections

Read the following passages in the *Catechism,* and ask the students to explain how the faith statements can be applied to this case:

- God plans for men and women to be good stewards of creation. (no. 373)
- The earth is endangered by poverty and violence. (no. 2402)
- The seventh commandment calls us to respect the integrity of creation. (no. 2415)

### Scripture Connections

*The Catholic Youth Bible* includes articles on the creation:

- "God Is Our Creator!" (see Genesis, chapters 1–2)
- "The Beauty of Creation" (see Phil 4.8–9)

### Course Connections

This case can be used with the course *Growing in Christian Morality* with the chapter on respect for creation:

- human beings as stewards of creation (pp. 230–231)
- appreciating creation (p. 236)
- taking care of creation (pp. 240–241)

## Research for Creation Case 1: Caring for the Environment

You can pursue further research on this topic by visiting the Web site provided by Environment Hawaii or by logging on to our Faith Community Builders Web site, *www.smp.org/hs,* and searching the links and resources provided there.

# The LISTEN Process Applied

Use the sample questions below to help the students work through the application of the LISTEN process for this case. You may wish to suggest questions for the students or focus on one particular section of the process.

## Look for the Facts

1. What critical decision did Leanne need to make once she learned about Kualoa Beach?
2. How was Kualoa Beach being destroyed?

## Imagine Possibilities

1. What are all the possible ways to handle this situation?
2. How could creativity have been used in handling this decision?
3. Are there any short- or long-term consequences for choosing to get involved or not?

## Seek Insight Beyond Your Own

1. What advice would your friends and family give you about getting involved in an environmental effort?
2. Is there a teacher or counselor at your school who could offer you guidance and support in making a decision like this?
3. Whom would you call to help you organize a clean-up effort like Leanne's? Do you believe that you would have a good response?

## Turn Inward

1. What would go through your mind if you saw a once beautiful beach polluted and becoming an eyesore?
2. What would motivate you to clean up the beach?
3. What would keep you from getting involved?
4. How would your conscience guide you in making a decision?

## Expect God's Help

1. Compose a prayer that you would pray with a group committed to cleaning up the environment.
2. Read Genesis 1:29–30. How might that Scripture reading comfort and challenge you if you were making a decision about getting involved in an environmental cleanup?

## Name Your Decision

1. What decision would you make if you were in Leanne's position?
2. What core values are being upheld in living out that decision?

## Final Questions and Thoughts on Creation Case 1: Caring for the Environment

1. Are there any agencies in your community that deal with local environmental issues?
2. What might be done with the money that is saved through simple living?
3. What lingering questions or thoughts do you have after reflecting on this case?

# Creation Case 1

## Caring for the Environment

Leanne Nakamura lives in Hawaii, the state most often described as paradise. When Leanne was a junior at Castle High School, she learned about the popular Kualoa Beach, which was being ruined by fishing nets washed ashore from boats. The nets were digging into the sand and sticking to the coral reefs offshore. This in turn was trapping and killing fish and sea turtles and endangering monk seals. Litter and dead fish were caught in the nets, causing a beautiful beach to be not only an eyesore but a threat to the area's ecosystems.

Leanne decided to do something about this. She called everyone she knew—friends, members of school clubs, and environmental groups—to get together to clean up Kualoa Beach. Just a few months later, Leanne, along with some other friends committed to action, formed a group called S.A.V.E., Student Actions and Values for the Environment.

Leanne was convinced that someone had to remind people of the environment's fragility. "It's hard to believe that something as beautiful as Hawaii could go bad," explained Leanne. "I think people here forget about the environment."

It took four weekends and seven truckloads to clean the beach of litter and fishnet. Kualoa Beach was finally clear and beautiful again. Leanne eventually earned a community spirit award for leading the efforts.

What's next for S.A.V.E.? A canal clogged by litter that has not been dredged for over twenty years. "It's really gross. If you have a cut and you get some of that water in it, it's going to get infected," according to Leanne.

Knowing that S.A.V.E. cannot solve all the problems of Hawaii's environment on its own, Leanne believes that her group can help by doing whatever it can. "We're trying to find little things to do," she explained. "People take this place for granted. They forget how special Hawaii is and how lucky they are to live here."

## Applying the LISTEN Process

Direct the students to their casebook, or photocopy and distribute the LISTEN process handout on page 209 for use with the students.

# Resources for Creation Case 2

## Concept Focus:
## Stewardship of the Earth's Resources, Living Simply

Throughout the discussion of the case, bring up the following points and have the students apply and reflect on them:
- We respect God's creation when we see all created things—living and nonliving—as good in themselves. *Ecological justice* involves the obligations that we as humans have to the rest of creation.
- We respect creation when we study and support the interconnected and dynamic balance within creation.
- We respect creation when we take care of it, as part of our efforts to build the Reign of God. Human beings are causing and tolerating widespread environmental damage to the earth and its atmosphere. Specific actions by individuals and groups can reverse and prevent such damage and make a huge impact on the future of the earth.

## *Catechism* Connections

Read the following passages in the *Catechism,* and ask the students to explain how the faith statements can be applied to this case:
- God plans for men and women to be good stewards of creation. (no. 373)
- The earth is endangered by poverty and violence. (no. 2402)
- The virtue of temperance requires us to practice moderate attachment to the world's goods. (no. 2407)
- The seventh commandment calls us to respect the integrity of creation. (no. 2415)

## Scripture Connections

*The Catholic Youth Bible* includes articles on stewardship and simple living:
- "Total Commitment" (see Mk 8.34–38)
- "Sacrificial Giving" (see Mk 12.41–44)
- "The Greed Trap" (see Lk 12.13–21)
- "Stewardship: Making a Contribution" (see Lk 21.1–4)

## Course Connections

This case can be used with the course *Growing in Christian Morality* with the chapter on respect for creation:
- human beings as stewards of creation (pp. 230–231)
- appreciating creation (p. 236)

## Research for Creation Case 2: Simple Living

You can pursue further research on this topic by searching the Web site run by the journal *Simple Living* or by logging on to our Faith Community Builders Web site, *www.smp.org/bs,* and searching the links and resources provided there.

# The LISTEN Process Applied

Use the sample questions below to help the students work through the application of the LISTEN process for this case. You may wish to suggest questions for the students or focus on one particular section of the process.

## Look for the Facts

1. What was the central decision facing James and Lois in how to live their life together?
2. What pressure is there to live the "American Dream?" What is that dream in terms of material goods and possessions?
3. How much money does it take to run a household?

## Imagine Possibilities

1. What options are possible in this situation?
2. How could creativity have been used in living simply?
3. Are there any short- or long-term consequences for choosing to live simply or accumulating material goods? (You may wish to use the consequence tree handout on page 208 for this activity.)

## Seek Insight Beyond Your Own

1. What advice would your family give you concerning how to live your life in terms of possessions?
2. Would your friends have respect for your decision to live simply?
3. Lois and James had a neighbor committed to simple living, and he served as a role model for them. Are there any neighbors or organizations in your area that would support this type of lifestyle?

## Turn Inward

1. What would go through your mind if your parents chose a more simple lifestyle for your family, possibly disconnecting the phone or radically decreasing the amount of water or energy consumption in your home?
2. What would motivate you to choose a simpler lifestyle?
3. What would keep you from cutting back on material possessions?
4. How would your conscience guide you in making a decision?

## Expect God's Help

1. Compose a prayer asking God for help in dealing with the materialism and greed so prevalent in our society.
2. Read Luke 12:22–34. How might that Scripture reading comfort and challenge you if you were making a decision whether to live more simply?

## Name Your Decision

1. What decision would you make if you were James or Lois? Would you choose the simpler lifestyle or live well within your means?
2. What core values are being upheld in living out that decision?

### Final Questions and Thoughts on Creation Case 2: Simple Living

1. Why is a decision to live simply so countercultural?
2. What are some ways that you could cut back on your consumption of water and energy?
3. How can living simply be a way of living out the virtue of respect for creation?
4. What lingering questions or thoughts do you have after reflecting on this case?

### Simple Living

Even though they made a combined salary of $70,000, James and Lois Sachs, both teachers, decided to build a house that reflected their own design and philosophy of life.

The small house includes a futon that the couple made by hand and some recycled items, such as a beauty-salon chair in the living room and a discarded ladder to their upstairs. The couple also uses a wood stove and heats shower water on it.

"You can do these things in the city, too," James said. "It's just basically cutting back." Cutting back means a monthly budget of $1000. They use only 20 gallons of water as opposed to the typical 120. They also spent an entire year without a phone. James recalled that being the quietest year of their life.

James and Lois have a neighbor named Ray Starrett who shares the same philosophy and works with the Wisconsin Greens, an environmental action group. His economical car has over 175,000 miles on it. He uses a smaller, portable plastic cooler powered by solar energy as opposed to a refrigerator that uses about half of the home's energy. Conscious of this, he also uses a long-lasting fluorescent light bulb in his lone living room lamp. James and Lois share meals with Ray weekly and believe that Ray has been an incredible influence in their life.

"We have friends that come out here and shake their head and say, 'You're not living the American dream,'" said James. "They are a little jealous because they are just more wrapped up in things."

"But they give us a lot of respect because of the courage we have to do what we thought," added Lois.

## Applying the LISTEN Process

Direct the students to their casebook, or photocopy and distribute the LISTEN process handout on page 209 for use with the students.

# Resources for Creation Case 3

**Trees Can Help**

## Concept Focus: Global Climatic Change

Throughout the discussion of the case, bring up the following points and have the students apply and reflect on them:

- We respect God's creation when we see all created things—living and nonliving—as good in themselves. *Ecological justice* involves the obligations that we as humans have to the rest of creation.
- We respect creation when we study and support the interconnected and dynamic balance within creation.
- We respect creation when we take care of it as part of our efforts to build the Reign of God. Human beings are causing and tolerating widespread environmental damage to the earth and its atmosphere. Specific actions by individuals and groups can reverse and prevent such damage and make a huge impact on the future of the earth.

## *Catechism* Connections

Read the following passages in the *Catechism,* and ask the students to explain how the faith statements can be applied to this case:

- God plans for men and women to be good stewards of creation. (no. 373)
- The earth is endangered by poverty and violence. (no. 2402)
- The virtue of temperance requires us to practice moderate attachment to the world's goods. (no. 2407)
- The seventh commandment calls us to respect the integrity of creation. (no. 2415)

## Scripture Connections

*The Catholic Youth Bible* includes articles on creation:

- "God Is Our Creator" (see Genesis, chapters 1–2)
- "The Beauty of Creation" (see Phil 4.8–9)

## Course Connections

This case can be used with the course *Growing in Christian Morality* with the chapter on respect for creation:

- human beings as stewards of creation (pp. 230–231)
- the problem of global climatic change (pp. 233–234)
- appreciating creation (p. 236)

## Research for Creation Case 3: Trees Can Help

You can pursue further research on this case by searching the Web site for the TreePeople organization or by logging on to our Faith Community Builders Web site, *www.smp.org/hs,* and searching the links and resources provided there.

# The LISTEN Process Applied

Use the sample questions below to help the students work through the application of the LISTEN process for this case. You may wish to suggest questions for the students or focus on one particular section of the process.

## Look for the Facts

1. How were the trees destroyed by pollution?
2. What decision did Andy face once he learned about the effects of smog on the forests?

## Imagine Possibilities

1. What are all the possible options for dealing with this knowledge?
2. How could creativity have been used in creating options for dealing with the trees dying from the smog?
3. Are there any short- or long-term consequences for choosing whether to get involved? (You may wish to use the consequence tree handout on page 208 for this activity.)

## Seek Insight Beyond Your Own

1. What advice would your friends and family give you about getting involved in an environmental effort?
2. Is there a teacher or counselor at your school who could offer you guidance and support in making a decision like this?
3. What types of organizations in your community could provide valuable information about the greenhouse effect, global warming, and deforestation?

## Turn Inward

1. What would go through your mind if you learned about the forests dying and you actually saw the effects of the smog on the trees?
2. What would motivate you to plant trees?
3. What would keep you from getting involved?
4. How would your conscience guide you in making a decision?

## Expect God's Help

1. Compose a prayer or blessing for trees that are dying.
2. Read Psalm 92:12–15. How might that Scripture reading comfort and challenge you if you were making a decision whether to get involved with an organization like TreePeople.

## Name Your Decision

1. What decision would you make if you had Andy's experiences?
2. What core values are being upheld in living out that decision?

### Final Questions and Thoughts on Creation Case 3: Trees Can Help

1. Is there a group in your area committed to reforestation?
2. Do you believe what Andy says about volunteerism, that it can heal just about everything?
3. What lingering questions or thoughts do you have after reflecting on this case?

# Creation Case 3

## Trees Can Help

In the early 1970s, Andy Lipkis was a high school student near Los Angeles. He went to a summer camp and learned how pollution was killing the forests in the area. The smog from Los Angeles drifted up to the San Bernardino Mountains and would actually choke the trees.

Andy took action. He organized other campers, and in three weeks of very hard work, they ripped up a parking lot and planted eight thousand redwood, cedar, and pine trees that are smog-resistant. "It was backbreaking work that required all of our creativity," said Andy.

It did not take long for the forest to come back to life. "We saw squirrels and birds playing on the land," he remembered. "We felt we had healed something."

The experience from those days in summer camp was a life-altering one that set Andy on his life's path. "When that summer was over, I knew I wanted to keep doing this. I wanted other kids to have this experience," he recalled.

Andy studied ecology and searched for ways to encourage people to plant more trees. Trees absorb carbon dioxide, and Andy sees this as an easy solution to the greenhouse effect and global warming. "Trees are like acupuncture needles," said Andy. "They help heal the Earth."

Andy started the environmental group TreePeople and began searching for ways to fund his organization. "I started a long process of trying and failing. Being able to fail is a key to the volunteer process," Andy believes. "In their jobs, people aren't allowed to do that. The real joy of being a volunteer is the freedom to express yourself without fear that it will be held against you."

Years later, Andy is still finding ways to save our planet. He has enlisted thousands of volunteers, and TreePeople is responsible for directly or indirectly planting more than 170 million trees worldwide. Whether sending fruit trees to Africa to help feed hungry people or teaching homeowners and city planners how trees can reduce the need for fossil fuels, Andy believes in people saving themselves by saving the land. "Our message is so far beyond trees. If the idea of volunteerism can be presented in the right way, I think it has the potential for healing everything."

## Applying the LISTEN Process

Direct the students to their casebook, or photocopy and distribute the LISTEN process handout on page 209 for use with the students.

# REVERENCE FOR LIFE
### Cherishing the Gift

# Theme Section Resources

## Discussion-Starter: Talk Tickets

*Vary the way you discuss and process the cases in your classroom. Try this idea during one of the cases in this section.*

When the students come into the classroom, give them each a ticket. Tell them that these will be used during large-group discussion.

When it comes time to discuss the case, you may wish to have small groups process a few questions to "warm up" and allow students who feel more comfortable in small groups to share.

If possible, set up the classroom in a semicircle or other arrangement that allows everyone to see one another. Explain that each ticket is worth one comment and that you will ask questions from the leader's guide to stimulate discussion. Once a student makes a comment, he or she must turn in the ticket and listen to everyone else.

If someone would choose not to participate and would like to give his or her ticket to another student, that is permissible as long as it is done discreetly. No student may receive more than one other ticket, and a particular student cannot speak more than two times total.

## Faith Application

After discussing the cases in this theme, ask the students to consider an action step that would move what they have learned out into the world. Consider these possibilities:

- finding out about bone marrow transplants and how to become a donor
- sponsoring a bone marrow donor pledge-a-thon
- becoming involved in a hospice program in the community
- starting a SADD (Students Against Drunken Driving) chapter at your school, or increasing its presence in the community

## Opening Prayer

*(See handout on next page.)*

# A Prayer for Reverence for Life

*All:* God of all life, be with us this day as we pray.

*Reader 1:* Maker of life, we pray for those on the edges of life.

*Reader 2:* The unborn.

*Reader 3:* The newly born.

*Reader 4:* The premature infant.

*Reader 5:* Those on life support.

*Reader 6:* Those in a coma.

*Reader 7:* Those who are dying.

*All:* Maker of life, be with those whose lives are fragile and need your care.

*Reader 1:* Giver of life, we pray for those whose lives are not valued.

*Reader 2:* The oppressed.

*Reader 3:* The abused.

*Reader 4:* Those living in war zones.

*Reader 5:* The imprisoned.

*Reader 6:* Children.

*Reader 7:* The elderly.

*All:* Giver of life, bring peace to those whose lives are ones of suffering. Touch our hearts so that we may reach out to them.

*Reader 1:* Sustainer of life, your spirit fills us and enlivens us.

*All:* May we reverence the precious gift of life.

*Reader 1:* Creator God, your breath stirred the dead to life.

*All:* May we rise to see the life that wants to live in us and in others. We ask this in the name of Jesus Christ. Amen.

# Resources for Reverence Case 1

Sisters for Life

## Concept Focus: Technology Dilemmas

Throughout the discussion of the case, bring up the following points and have the students apply and reflect on them:

- The Catholic church holds that human life is a sacred gift that is to be cared for by us until physical life reaches its natural end.
- Every child is a gift of God and is equal in dignity to his or her parents. Contraceptive techniques may lead parents to view themselves as the gift-givers.
- The church's "consistent ethic of life" means life is to be reverenced from "womb to tomb."
- Modern developments in medical technology have created possibilities for controlling human life that must be approached with ethical vigilance.

## *Catechism* Connections

Read the following passages in the *Catechism,* and ask the students to explain how the faith statements can be applied to this case:

- A child is a gift of God; its dignity is not owed to the child serving as a means to some end. (no. 1887)
- Human life is sacred. (no. 2258)
- Advances in science and medicine can contribute to healing the sick and to advancing public health. (no. 2292)
- There must be guiding principles in scientific research. (no. 2294)
- Research and experiments must respect the dignity of the person. (no. 2295)
- Organ transplants are moral when there is proportionate good. (no. 2296)
- A child is a gift. (no. 2378)

## Scripture Connections

*The Catholic Youth Bible* includes articles on the sacredness of life:

- "Brothers and Sisters" (see Gen 4.9)
- "The Sacredness of Life" (see Psalm 139)

## Course Connections

This case can be used with the course *Growing in Christian Morality* with the chapter on reverence for life:
- consistent ethic of life (p. 247)
- medical technology dilemmas (pp. 247–248)

## Research for Reverence Case 1: Sisters for Life

This case deals with the need for a bone marrow transplant. Marrow is found inside the body's bones. It contains stem cells that produce red blood cells, white blood cells, and platelets. Anissa Ayala's disease, chronic myelogenous leukemia, involved a change in the chromosomes of bone marrow cells, and so a bone marrow transplant would enable new healthy marrow cells to grow.

You can pursue further research on this topic by searching the Web site provided by the Bone Marrow Donors Worldwide organization or by logging on to our Faith Community Builders Web site, *www.smp.org/hs,* and searching the links and resources provided there.

## Follow-up for Reverence Case 1: Sisters for Life

The Anissa Foundation is committed to public awareness of the issues raised in this case. Anissa herself is a cofounder and works with the foundation. Its Web site contains more information about her story, the foundation, leukemia, and bone marrow transplantation. The site also contains pictures of Marissa and Anissa today.

# The LISTEN Process Applied

Use the sample questions below to help the students work through the application of the LISTEN process for this case. You may wish to suggest questions for the students or focus on one particular section of the process.

## Look for the Facts

1. What were the critical decisions Anissa faced? What critical decisions did Anissa's parents face?
2. What was the key moral decision in this case?
3. Was there an element of time involved with Anissa's medical condition?

## Imagine Possibilities

1. What would you do if you found out that you had a life-threatening disease that could possibly kill you in a couple years? What options did Anissa have for medical treatment?
2. What were the potential consequences for each option? (You may wish to use the consequence tree handout from page 208 for this activity.)

## Seek Insight Beyond Your Own

1. Whom would you turn to for advice if you were in a situation like Anissa's? Why?
2. Whom would you turn to for advice if you were the parents of a child who could die without a transplant? Why?
3. Read these quotes doctors made about this case. Do these statements bring new insight into the decision made in this case? How?
   - "Children aren't medicine for other people. Children are themselves." (George Annas, professor at Boston University's medical school)
   - "This was not bringing a donor into the world. This was bringing a child into the world who may potentially be a donor." (Dr. Steven Foreman, Anissa's doctor)
   - "When you have a little child who's going to be a donor of an organ like bone marrow, you have a sense that the child is being created for that purpose and really doesn't participate in that choice, and so it's more troubling. I think it's a kind of act which, in a desire to respect life and a desire to save life, turns human life into a means rather than an end in itself." (Alexander Capron, medical ethicist and professor at the University of Southern California)

4. The church document *Instruction on Respect for Human Life in Its Origin and the Dignity of Human Reproduction* gives four guiding principles when considering moral issues involved with medical technology. How could each of these principles bring new insight to the decision to conceive another child and then use that child as a bone marrow donor?

   - Life is a gift from God. We must appreciate its "inestimable value."
   - Science and technology must be used to benefit all people.
   - We are both body and spirit—a "unified totality."
   - Just because a procedure is "technically possible" does not make it "morally admissible."

## Turn Inward

1. If you were the parents of a chronically sick child like Anissa, would you consider conceiving another child in the hope that he or she would be a match for the older child? What would motivate you to consider this option?
2. How would you feel if your parents made the decision that Anissa's parents did? Why?
3. On a pure gut level, how do you feel about this case?

## Expect God's Help

1. Compose a prayer that you would pray if your child were undergoing a very serious operation.
2. Read Psalm 8. How might that Scripture reading comfort and challenge you if you were making decisions like the ones in this case?

## Name Your Decision

1. What decision would you make if you were one of Anissa's parents? Why?
2. What core values are being upheld in living out that decision?

### Final Questions and Thoughts on Reverence Case 1: Sisters for Life

1. Whom do you most identify with in this case? Why?
2. Imagine that you were in Marissa's position. How would you feel about being a donor for your sister? How would you feel about the circumstances surrounding your conception?
3. Is each human life held sacred in this case?

4. What may have motivated the person who was going to donate his or her bone marrow to back out of that decision? What did you think about this? Did this person have a moral obligation to donate his or her marrow? Why or why not?

5. Some medical researchers believe that transplants of fetal tissue may help lessen the symptoms of or even cure diseases such as Parkinson's disease or juvenile diabetes. Do you believe that could lead to babies being conceived and then aborted to provide fetal tissue? Explain your thoughts fully.

6. What lingering questions or thoughts do you have after reflecting on this case?

## Sisters for Life

Anissa Ayala was an athletic teenager with a steady boyfriend, loving family, and ordinary problems, living in Walnut, California, in 1987. When she started having painful stomach cramps and found strange lumps forming around her ankles, Anissa chose not to tell her parents because she was afraid she may have to get a blood test. Just thinking about going to the doctor made her nervous, and she had always hated needles. But the pain grew more severe and, right after Anissa turned sixteen, she found herself in the hospital having tests. The frightening diagnosis—she had chronic myelogenous leukemia, a fast-growing malignant cancer of the bone marrow. Anissa and her family were told that the disease would kill her within a few years if she did not have a bone marrow transplant.

Family members, especially siblings, have a greater chance than unrelated persons to be a match for a bone marrow transplant. Anissa's mother, father, brother, and extended family were tested, but no matches were found. The family worked with the National Bone Marrow Donor Registry and discovered the odds of finding a perfect match were one in twenty thousand.

Anissa dealt with her disease by remaining as calm as possible and seeking to understand as much as she could about it. Her parents, Abe and Mary, were stricken with grief and sadness. Her mother said: "At the beginning, the stress was really bad. I was trying to stay 'up' for her, and she was trying to stay 'up' for me. She would look at me, and I would start crying." Her father had similar feelings. "The first thing you think is, 'She's going to die,'" he said. "I started getting flashbacks to when she was a little girl. I remember going into her room at home when she was in the hospital and thinking that maybe she'd never come back. It's really hard on the heart."

Even though Anissa responded well to early chemotherapy treatments, the family knew that a bone marrow transplant was their only hope for a cure. A match was found at one point, but the donor backed out. The family was devastated.

Mary, age forty-three, and Abe, age forty-five, had thought of having another child once before, but Abe had had a vasectomy sixteen years earlier. With Anissa's life hanging in the balance, they decided to try to conceive, knowing that a sibling has a one-in-four chance of being a life-saving bone marrow donor. Abe underwent a procedure to reverse his vasectomy and, six months later, Mary became pregnant with a baby girl. Amniocentesis and tissue-typing tests confirmed the baby would be a match for Anissa.

Much controversy surrounded the decision to conceive a child to be a donor for another. Medical ethicists argued that it was wrong, while the

Ayala family said the conception was in the spirit of love. Anissa did speak out on the issue saying, "She's my baby sister, and we're going to love her for who she is, not for what she can give to me." Mary Ayala commented that the child began healing Anissa, even while in the womb: "She has given Anissa more of a reason to live."

In April 1990, Marissa Eve Ayala was born to a family who embraced her birth and called her their "miracle baby." The chose the name Marissa because it combined Mary and Anissa's names; they chose the middle name Eve because it means "giver of life."

Fourteen months later, Anissa had chemotherapy and radiation to kill the cancer and her marrow. Bone marrow was taken from Marissa's hip, then transplanted into Anissa intravenously. Two hours after her operation, Marissa was running up and down hospital corridors. Given a 70 percent chance of survival, Anissa spent six weeks in the hospital.

Anissa did recover and is now considered cured. She was married one year and one day after the transplant. Marissa was the flower girl and danced at the wedding. Anissa will never be able to have her own biological children due to the chemotherapy she received, but according to her mother, "she considers Marissa like her own child."

Some have commented that there is a very special, unspoken bond between the two sisters. Anissa says: "Oh! She's a piece of me. She's my heart and my soul. I mean, that little girl has given me something that I can't give back. You know, I can't give life back to her, and so I can only give her the best life possible. And that's what I want to do. She's a special gift that has really been given to us."

Anissa works as an advocate for bone marrow transplantation and has established a foundation to provide support to others who are suffering from leukemia or other diseases and need bone marrow transplants.

## Applying the LISTEN Process

Direct the students to their casebook, or photocopy and distribute the LISTEN process handout on page 209 for use with the students.

## Mother and Daughter

### Concept Focus: Surrogate Parenting

Throughout the discussion of the case, discuss the following points from the text with the students:

- *Consistent ethic of life* means life is to be reverenced from "womb to tomb."
- Modern developments in medical technology have created possibilities for controlling human life that must be approached with ethical vigilance.
- On the issue of birth control, the church holds that responsible family planning is acceptable if the methods used do not disrupt the nature of sexual intercourse.
- The technologies of surrogate parenthood present a particular challenge to an ethic that reverences the sacredness of human life.

### *Catechism* Connections

Read the following passages in the *Catechism,* and ask the students to explain how the faith statements can be applied to this case:

- There must be guiding principles in scientific research. (no. 2294)
- Researching ways to reduce human sterility is to be encouraged if it is according to God's design and will. (no. 2375)
- Medical techniques used that involve the "dissociation" of husband and wife are immoral. (no. 2376)
- Medical techniques that involve the "dissociation" of husband and wife are gravely immoral. (no. 2376)
- Techniques that dissociate the sexual act from procreation are morally unacceptable. (no. 2377)
- Every child has the right to be respected as a person and as the fruit of conjugal love from the moment of conception. (no. 2378)
- Physical sterility is not an absolute evil. (no. 2379)

### Scripture Connections

Explain to the students that having children was the primary role of women in the Scriptures. It was seen as a great blessing to have children; likewise, it was seen as a curse to not have children. Some of the women even offered their maidservants to their husbands so that children could be conceived. Have the students read the stories of the biblical women who were once infertile, and then discuss them.

- Genesis 16:1–4, 18:9–15, 21:1–7 (Sarah)
- Genesis 25:21–26 (Rebekah)

- Genesis 29:31–35 (Leah)
- Genesis 30:1–24 (Rachel)
- Luke 1:36–45 (Elizabeth)

## Course Connections

This case can be used with the course *Growing in Christian Morality* with the chapter on reverence for life:
- consistent ethic of life (p. 247)
- medical technology dilemmas (pp. 247–248)
- surrogate parenting (pp. 254–255)

## Research for Reverence Case 2: Mother and Daughter

It may be helpful to discuss some of the medical issues involved in this case, primarily the inability of Christa to have children because she was born without a uterus. Review the functions of the female reproductive system with the students as necessary, particularly the role of the ovaries and the uterus.

For information about surrogate parenting, research a few of the many Web sites that promote surrogate parenting or log on to our Faith Community Builders Web site, *www.smp.org/hs,* and searching the links and resources provided there.

Other controversial cases involving surrogate parenting may also provide interesting discussion for classes. Consider investigating the story of Mary Beth Whitehead-Gould, the mid-1980s case that brought the issue of surrogate parenting into the public eye. "Baby M" became the center of a fierce legal battle when Mary Beth changed her mind about turning over the baby she carried for another couple.

# The LISTEN Process Applied

Use the sample questions below to help the students work through the application of the LISTEN process for this case. You may wish to suggest questions for the students or focus on one particular section of the process.

## Look for the Facts

1. What were the key moral issues that Christa and Arlette faced in this case?
2. What facts need to be known in order to make a good, moral decision?

## Imagine Possibilities

1. What options did Christa have for having children one day?
2. List all the possible approaches a couple has in dealing with infertility.
3. What is the most loving response Arlette could have had in this situation? (You may wish to use the consequence tree handout on page 208 for this activity.)
3. What potential consequences could you foresee down the road for Christa? Arlette? Kevin? Dan? the children?

## Seek Insight Beyond Your Own

1. Whom would you turn to for advice if you were faced with the prospect of not having children down the road?
2. What advice would your family and friends give you if you were infertile?
3. The four principles from the church document *Instruction on Respect for Human Life in Its Origin and the Dignity of Human Reproduction* can be applied to this case. How could each of these principles bring new insight to the decision to become a surrogate parent?
   - Life is a gift from God. We must appreciate its "inestimable value."
   - Science and technology must be used to benefit all people.
   - We are both body and spirit—a "unified totality."
   - Just because a procedure is "technically possible" does not make it "morally admissible."

## Turn Inward

1. How would you feel if you found out today, as a teenager, that you would not be able to have children? How would you feel if you were engaged and your partner was unable to have children? Explain fully.
2. What intuitive sense do you have about this case?
3. How would you explain to the twins the circumstances of their birth?

## Expect God's Help

1. Imagine that you were a hospital chaplain at the hospital where Arlette was preparing to deliver the babies. Compose a prayer that you would pray with Christa as her mother was being prepared for the cesarean section.
2. Read Psalm 113. How could that Scripture reading comfort and challenge you if you were making decisions like Christa's and Arlette's?

## Name Your Decision

1. Would you decide to become a surrogate mother for your son or daughter's baby? Why or why not?
2. What core values are being upheld in living out that decision?

## Final Questions and Thoughts on Reverence Case 2: Mother and Daughter

1. Whom do you most identify with in this case? Why?
2. Was the consistent ethic of life upheld in this situation?
3. Was the dignity of every human upheld in this case? Apply it specifically to Christa, Arlette, and the children.
4. Reinforce the two purposes of sexual intercourse as discussed in the student text, page 251. How can these purposes be applied in this case?
5. Do these technological advances increase the temptation for humans to "play God?"
6. What do you think the future will hold in the area of reproductive technology? How do you believe people should go about deciding the morality of future medical and technological advances in this area?
7. Arlette Schweitzer said she had no doubts about her decision. She has said: "If you can give the gift of life, why not? If medical science affords that opportunity, why not take it?" How would you personally respond to Arlette?

8. Surrogate parenting has been an issue in the courts and with medical ethicists. Is it morally right to pay someone to be a surrogate? Would it be more acceptable if someone was a surrogate for free? What happens if the surrogate changes her mind? How would you decide these issues legally? How would you decide these issues morally?

9. What lingering questions or thoughts do you have after reflecting on this case?

# Reverence Case 2

## Mother and Daughter

When Christa Uchytil was fourteen years old, doctors discovered that she was born without a uterus. "I knew it meant I couldn't have children—no one had to tell me," she said. Christa was devastated because she had always assumed that she would be a mom. But Christa's mom, Arlette, was optimistic: "Don't worry," she told Christa. "By the time you're ready, they'll have something. Science moves fast."

Two years later Christa's parents took her to the Mayo Clinic in Rochester, Minnesota, for a consultation. The doctor informed them that Christa's eggs were fine, but that she would not be able to carry a baby to term. Arlette had joked with the doctor about transplanting her own uterus. When the doctor asked how old she was, the idea of Arlette's carrying Christa's babies occurred to both women.

Four years later Christa met Kevin Uchytil. She told him on their third date about her problem. He was impressed that Arlette would carry a baby for her daughter. Christa and Kevin were married a year later and, after waiting a year, Christa and her mom started taking drugs to synchronize their menstrual cycles. Arlette had to endure painful hormone injections for eighty-nine days. She still has scars on both her hips, but said that "as long as you know there's an end to it, I think you can bear almost anything."

A month later eggs were taken from Christa's ovaries and fertilized with Kevin's sperm. Four eggs were then implanted into Arlette's uterus. "I sat on the nest, but they were Christa's eggs," said Arlette.

Ten days later Arlette called her daughter and son-in-law and told them, "Congratulations! You're pregnant." Early into the pregnancy, doctors discovered that Arlette was carrying twins. Christa and Kevin were ecstatic.

On 12 October 1991, Arlette delivered a baby boy and a baby girl by cesarean section, with Christa right by her side. There were no complications for Arlette or the twins.

Arlette and her husband, Dan, are Roman Catholics, and both believe that doing this was meant to be. "I think it must have been in God's plan for us to have had our children so young so I'd be young enough to have these babies for our daughter," said Arlette. "Family is everything to us," explains Dan Shweitzer.

Arlette said that she has no regrets and would do it again. Christa and Kevin, however, are not in any rush. "I have my babies, my husband, my home," said Christa. "It's perfect, all I'll ever want or need."

## Applying the LISTEN Process

Direct the students to their casebook, or photocopy and distribute the LISTEN process handout on page 209 for use with the students.

**A Time to Die**

## Concept Focus: Euthanasia

Throughout the discussion of the case, discuss the following points from the text with the students:

- When the Catholic church speaks of euthanasia, it means a specific act or omission done intentionally to directly cause death in a patient, thus relieving the person of all suffering. The Catholic church considers euthanasia to be a grave evil.
- "Consistent ethic of life" means that life is to be reverenced from "womb to tomb."
- Even though a person's life may seem burdensome or useless, no one has the right to intentionally take that life.
- Compassion can be tough when it means sharing another's pain. In compassion we do not kill someone whose suffering we cannot bear.
- The Catholic church teaches that we are not obligated to accept or continue medical treatment that is disproportionate (out of proportion) to the good that can be done.
- If legalized, euthanasia could create great pressure for ill people to end their life.

## *Catechism* Connections

Read the following passages from the *Catechism,* and ask the students to explain how the faith statements can be applied to this case:

- Sick and handicapped people deserve respect and should be helped to live a normal life. (no. 2276)
- Direct euthanasia is morally unacceptable. (no. 2277)
- Refusal of "over-zealous" treatment can be morally legitimate. (no. 2278)
- Ordinary care must continue even if death is imminent. (no. 2279)

## Scripture Connections

*The Catholic Youth Bible* includes articles on suffering and grief that are relevant to this case:

- "Reading Plan 7: Why Do We Suffer?" (see "Suggested Reading Plans" section)
- "Surviving Grief" (see 2 Sam 18.33—19.8)
- "Praying for Death?" (see Tobit, chapter 3)
- "In Good Times and Bad" (see Job 1.13–21)
- "Being There" (see Job 2.11–13)
- "Our Cross to Bear" (see Psalm 6)

## Course Connections

This case can be used with the course *Growing in Christian Morality* with the chapter on reverence for life:
- consistent ethic of life (p. 247)
- medical technology dilemmas (pp. 247–248)
- killing versus letting go (p. 258)
- proportionate treatment (p. 259)

## Research for Reverence Case 3: A Time to Die

Give the students some background on the symptoms of a persistent vegetative state so they can better understand Christine's condition. It may also be helpful to explain the role and function of a feeding tube.
- For a legal perspective, look at the American Bar Association's Web site.
- Ask the students to find out about living wills. A good Web site to look at is the U.S. Living Will Registry.
- Encourage the students to talk with their parents about what their wishes would be in a situation like Christine's.
- Have the students research other cases similar to Christine's, such as Karen Quinlan's, Nancy Kruzan's, and Hugh Finn's.
- Encourage the students to look at the controversy and legal battles of Jack Kevorkian.

You can pursue further research by logging on to our Faith Community Builders Web site, *www.smp.org/hs,* and searching the links and resources provided there.

# The LISTEN Process Applied

Use the sample questions below to help the students work through the application of the LISTEN process for this case. You may wish to suggest questions for the students or focus on one particular section of the process.

## Look for the Facts

1. What is the critical decision to be made by Christine's father, Peter Busalacchi?
2. What information would you need to know in order to make a good decision in a situation like this?
3. What other case had striking similarities to Christine Busalacchi's? How did it affect the political climate of the time?

## Imagine Possibilities

1. What options did Peter Busalacchi have for Christine's treatment? (You may wish to use the consequence tree handout on page 208 for this activity.)
2. How did the involvement of the state officials affect Christine and her family in the short- and long-term?
3. If you were the parent of Christine, what would be the most loving response you could make? Why?

## Seek Insight Beyond Your Own

1. If you had a loved one in Christine's situation, to whom would you first turn for advice? Why? Is there anyone else you would speak with? Why?
2. What legal issues were involved in this case?
3. What role and responsibility do you believe the state, government, legal system should play in cases like Christine's? Why?
4. The church gives some guidelines that can be applied to Christine's story. How might these statements bring new insight to this case?
   - Catholic teaching states that we are not obligated to accept or continue medical treatment that is out of proportion to the good that can be done by the treatment.
   - We have the right to die naturally, peacefully, and with dignity.

## Turn Inward

1. How would you feel if you had a loved one in Christine's situation?
2. If you were Christine's parents, what would your motives be for wishing to remove her feeding tube?
3. Put yourself in Christine's situation. What would you want your family to do if you were in a persistent vegetative state?

## Expect God's Help

1. If you were the clinic's chaplain where Christine was staying and you saw the anguish of the family, what prayer would you share with them?
2. Read Psalm 23. How could that Scripture reading provide comfort for the family?

## Name Your Decision

1. What decision would you make if you were in Peter Busalacchi's situation?
2. What core values are being upheld in living out that decision?

### Final Questions and Thoughts on Reverence Case 3: A Time to Die

1. Whom do you most identify with in this case? Why?
2. Did Christine's father show reverence for her life? Did the media? the legal system? the activists?
3. Did the media handle the case responsibly? Explain your thoughts fully.
4. If you were the manager of the local television station and had obtained a copy of the videotape, what options would you consider?
5. How would you have handled this situation as the administrator of the hospital where the protestors and the media showed up?
6. How would you have handled this if you were the state attorney general?
7. Elizabeth McDonald strongly believed that Christine's feeding tube should not be removed and chose to go to court to become her guardian. What other choices did she have?
8. Was the removal of Christine's feeding tube an example of a disproportionate treatment?
9. Did Christine die naturally, peacefully, and with dignity?
10. What lingering questions or thoughts do you have after reflecting on this case?

## A Time to Die

In May 1987 Christine Busalacchi was a vibrant and outgoing junior at Parkway West High School in a suburb of Saint Louis, Missouri. The evening of 29 May, she and a friend, Michael Allen, were driving to a party in a nearby town. Michael was driving Christine's car that night and was speeding. He ran a stop sign and crashed into another car.

The impact killed Michael. A police officer witnessed the accident and pulled Christine from the wreckage after the car caught on fire.

At the hospital doctors determined that Christine suffered from severe head injuries. The swelling in her brain was so severe that surgeons had to remove a large part of it. During this operation they also inserted a feeding tube in her stomach because she had lost the abilities to chew and swallow.

Over the next several months, doctors examined Christine to evaluate her condition. At least six neurologists diagnosed her as being in a PVS or persistent vegetative state. This is a chronic, irreversible condition caused by brain damage, and it meant that Christine would never think or feel again.

Five months after the accident, Christine was moved from the hospital to the Missouri Rehabilitation Center. Her father, Peter Busalacchi, and the rest of her family remained hopeful and wished for marked improvement in her condition. They loved "Chris" and participated in her care.

Three years passed, and the doctors told Peter Busalacchi that Christine would never regain an awareness of her environment. After hearing this Peter decided to remove Christine's feeding tube so that she could die.

Elsewhere in Missouri national attention was focused on a similar case. The family of a young woman named Nancy Cruzan sought to remove her feeding tube. Nancy had been in a PVS for many years following a serious car accident. State officials intervened and fought the family's decision all the way to the Supreme Court. The family was eventually allowed to make the decision to remove the feeding tube after they provided "clear and convincing" evidence that it would have been Nancy's wish. On 26 December 1990, twelve days after her feeding tube was removed, Nancy Cruzan died.

Because Christine was a patient at the same facility as Nancy, Peter Busalacchi was very aware of the media attention surrounding the Cruzan case. Peter decided to move his daughter to a Minnesota clinic where the legal climate was less politically charged. There the decision to remove a patient's feeding tube was made by families and doctors. Three days after

Nancy Cruzan's death, Peter planned to remove Christine from the Missouri facility. When he arrived at the center to move her, he was stopped by state troopers and a court order.

Over the next few months, the attention surrounding the Busalacchi case intensified. The governor and attorney general led Missouri's efforts. State officials released a videotape of Christine made by staff members at the rehabilitation center. On the tape, Christine appeared to laugh at jokes and move her leg on command. Soon the tape was playing on local television, and public opinion was divided.

A neurologist who saw the tape said the "automatic, involuntary behaviors of people in vegetative states could look like evidence of human awareness when shown on edited videotape."

In response to Christine's seeming awareness on the videotape, various statements surfaced to provide medical facts. Dr. Kenneth Smith, a neurosurgeon at Saint Louis University School of Medicine, said, "It's confusing for lay people because these people's eyes are open and they look like they are alert." Another doctor explained that this is a reason why PVS can be "an unnerving state." A statement from a hospital said that a person in a PVS could sometimes "make chewing movements and show brief smiles or grimaces. All of these actions, however, are involuntary and do not reflect a conscious awareness of self or the environment."

As the legal process continued, Peter Busalacchi had Christine moved to another Missouri state facility. More doctors and neurologists examined Christine and, while some claimed their tests inconclusive, most reached the same PVS diagnosis of previous doctors.

Satisfied by the medical evidence, a judge ruled that Peter had the right to determine his daughter's medical care and could move his daughter from Missouri. The appeal went before the state's Supreme Court in September of 1992. When a new attorney general took office in January of 1993, a motion was filed with the U.S. Supreme Court to dismiss the case. The highest court in the land did just that, leaving Peter free to decide Christine's future medical care.

Three days after the Supreme Court's decision, a woman with no relationship to the Bussalacchis went to court requesting that she become Christine's legal guardian. This woman, Elizabeth McDonald, was an anti-abortion activist in the Saint Louis area. The courts rejected her motion and upheld Peter's rights as Christine's father and legal guardian.

Peter moved Christine to Barnes Hospital, a private facility where another team of doctors concurred with the PVS diagnosis saying Christine was oblivious to pain, discomfort, and other stimuli, including her father.

On 1 March 1993, a group called We Are Concerned for the Handicapped attempted to apply federal disability laws to the case, saying it was discriminatory to remove Christine's feeding tube. Some activists claimed that she was simply disabled and that "removing her feeding was equivalent to murder." During this same time period, people protested outside the hospital, which received over 750 calls saying that the facility and its doctors were "murderers." Their efforts to apply federal disability laws in Christine's case failed. The Busalacchi family was now free to remove her feeding tube.

In the early morning of 7 March 1993, Peter Busalacchi was called to his daughter's bedside. He stroked her hair. Shortly after Christine was pronounced dead.

The family released a statement to the media that thanked people for their thoughts and prayers and asked for their understanding. "We know that we lost Chris the night of her car accident. We love you, Chris, and hope you found peace."

## Applying the LISTEN Process

Direct the students to their casebook, or photocopy and distribute the LISTEN process handout on page 209 for use with the students.

# Resources for Reverence Case 4

**Driving to Death**

## Concept Focus: Drinking and Driving

Throughout the discussion of the case, bring up the following points and have the students apply and reflect upon them:

- "Consistent ethic of life" means that life is to be reverenced from "womb to tomb."
- A car is the most powerful tool that most of us will ever operate, and it needs to be treated, it's been said, as a potentially unguided missile of one or two tons, equipped with combustible material.
- Driving under the influence of alcohol or drugs is like cocking the trigger of a loaded gun. Driving under the influence of alcohol or other drugs yourself or letting someone else do so indicates a terrible disregard for life.

## *Catechism* Connections

Read the following passages in the *Catechism,* and ask the students to explain how the faith statements can be applied to this case:

- Our life and health is a gift from God that deserves our care. (no. 2288)
- Temperance is a virtue. (no. 2290)

## Scripture Connections

*The Catholic Youth Bible* includes articles on alcohol, addictive behavior, and grief:

- "Surviving Grief" (see 2 Sam 18.33—19.8)
- "Dead Drunk!" (see Jdt 12.16—13.10)
- "A Tragic Tale" (see Sir 31.25–31)
- "Addictive Behavior" (see 1 Cor 10.6–14)
- "Alcohol" (see Eph 5.10–20)

## Course Connections

This case can be used with the course *Growing in Christian Morality* with the chapter on reverence for life:

- consistent ethic of life (p. 247)
- recklessly endangering human life (pp. 266 and 268)

## Research for Reverence Case 4: Driving to Death

It may be helpful to provide the students with up-to-date statistics on drinking and driving. You can pursue further research on this topic by searching the site provided by the Mothers Against Drunk Driving organization or by logging on to our Faith Community Builders Web site, *www.smp.org/hs,* and searching the links and resources provided there.

## Follow-up Activities for Reverence Case 4: Driving to Death

- Invite students who are involved in anti-drinking groups—SADD for example—or groups that promote healthy decisions to lead a discussion in class.
- Ask someone from the justice system (a police officer or lawyer) to speak on drinking and driving.
- Ask an emergency room nurse, doctor, or paramedic to come to class and speak about the realities of drinking and driving.

## Follow-up Information for Reverence Case 4: Driving to Death

- Verona High School lost another student, Nebyou Checol, to drinking and driving less than a month after Ryan Goldsmith died. What type of resources and support do you think the students of the high school and the local community would need?
- Ryan's mother sued the convenience store where Ryan got the beer that contributed to his fatal accident. According to the lawsuit, one of Ryan's friends bought the alcohol and then shared it with Ryan. All the boys were underage.

# The LISTEN Process Applied

Use the sample questions below to help the students work through the application of the LISTEN process for this case. You may wish to suggest questions for the students or focus on one particular section of the process.

## Look for the Facts

1. If you were a reporter for Verona High School's newspaper, what headline would you use for this story? Why?
2. What decisions did Ryan make that led to his accident?
3. Why did Ryan and his friends drink so much?
4. What different approaches did the parents take to their teens' drinking? Which of those were successful?

## Imagine Possibilities

1. How could Ryan and his friends have had a good time without alcohol? Brainstorm at least ten activities that are fun and safe.
2. What potential short- and long-term consequences are there for drinking and driving? (You may wish to use the consequence tree handout on page 208 for this activity.)

## Seek Insight Beyond Your Own

1. If you had a friend with a drinking problem, what would you do? Whom would you go to for advice? Why?
2. What programs at your school encourage healthy decisions involving alcohol? Do you and other students really listen to the speakers involved in those programs? Why or why not?
3. Mr. Goldsmith was trying to talk with and reach Ryan after Brian's serious accident. What could a parent say or do that would convince a teen to stop drinking heavily? Explain your answer.
4. What support systems or agencies are available in your area for people with drinking problems and those who love them? What types of programs are available?

## Turn Inward

1. How would you feel if you survived an automobile crash in which drinking was involved and the driver of the vehicle died? How would you cope with this?
2. What do you believe motivates Mr. Goldsmith to speak to teens about Ryan and his death? If you heard him speak, would you change your behavior? Why or why not?
3. What are your "blind spots" about drinking and driving?
4. What experiences may have shaped Ryan's drinking habits? How are your decisions regarding alcohol shaped by your experiences?
5. What do you think motivated Ryan's friends to create a "shrine" where empty beer cans could be left in his memory?

## Expect God's Help

1. Compose a prayer that would have been appropriate for Ryan's memorial service.
2. Read Galatians 5:16–21 and Ephesians 5:10–20. What do those Scripture readings have to say about drinking? What could they have taught Ryan and his friends? What can they teach you and your friends about the choices God wants us to make?

## Name Your Decision

1. Would you have made the decision to get in the truck with Ryan? Why or why not?
2. Would you have participated in leaving empty beer cans at the crash site or showing up drunk at Ryan's funeral? Explain why or why not.

### Final Questions and Thoughts on Reverence Case 4: Driving to Death
1. Whom do you most identify with in this case? Why?
2. What moral responsibility should be placed on the store clerk who sold alcohol to the underage boys? Why?
3. How did Ryan's "friends" react to his death? How did they cope with it? Would you consider those responses healthy ones? Why or why not?
4. In what ways could the school respond to Brian's accident and Ryan's death? Which of those ways would be most effective and why?
5. Analyze the degree of moral responsibility for each of the following: Ryan, Ryan's friends, parents, icy road conditions, store clerk who sold alcohol to the boys, society, the school. Who do you believe holds the most responsibility. Why?
6. What lingering questions or thoughts do you have after reflecting on this case?

# Reverence Case 4

## Driving to Death

Ryan Goldsmith was an outgoing and popular student at Verona High School in Madison, Wisconsin, where he was a senior and captain of the hockey team in the spring of 1995. Ryan was also a big drinker and loved to party with his friends.

Obtaining alcohol was not a problem for Ryan and his friends, even though they were underage. They knew of a small country store where the clerk did not ask for identification. Or there were always fake IDs available or someone over twenty-one willing to purchase alcohol for the underagers. Some of Ryan's friends had parents who allowed them to keep refrigerators stocked with beer in their basement. One parent explained this by saying, "We don't condone it, but if he's going to drink, we'd rather [have] him drink at home."

In February Ryan was at a party with his friends, including a boy named Brian Gehrke. After drinking, Brian decided to leave with two other boys, Jason and Roberto, because the party was getting boring. Jason drove his mom's pickup truck. It was icy outside, and none of the boys wore seatbelts. The truck crashed, and the impact threw Brian from the vehicle. Brian was seriously injured and in a coma for six weeks. The left side of his brain was damaged, leaving him with slurred speech and short-term memory loss.

Brian said that he and his friends started drinking because it was fun. His parents thought it started because school was not a source of motivation for the boys and they didn't feel part of the college crowd. But after the accident, Brian said he would never drink again.

Ryan's dad, Jim Goldsmith, was aware of his own son's drinking. "I was working on him. When Brian got hit, I told him: 'This is what I've been talking about. This is what could happen to you.' I was trying to use what happened to Brian Gehrke as an example." Mr. Goldsmith believed Ryan was starting to hear the message and said that others were talking to Ryan as well. "A very close friend and Ryan's girlfriend were encouraging him to slow down. He knew that they were right," said Mr. Goldsmith.

A month later Ryan and two friends drove out to a deserted housing development. After Ryan and his friends had a few beers, they decided to go to another friend's house. Ryan was known for his speeding and enjoyed the "rush of a car shooting you down the road." He drove very fast on the way to the friend's house and missed a turn. The truck ended up in a ditch after rolling on its side, and Ryan was trapped inside. None of the boys were wearing seatbelts. Ryan's friends, Tim and Roberto, were not seriously injured, but Ryan's skull was crushed.

Upon hearing news of the accident, Mr. Goldsmith rushed to the hospital. "I was scared but, even as scared as I was, I wasn't prepared for what I saw. The blood was pouring out of his left ear. Ryan was hooked up to various medical equipment to help him breathe. They were pumping blood into him. There was a lot of blood. It's an overwhelming, awful feeling when you see your son on the table, knowing he's going to die."

Ryan was pronounced dead at eleven o'clock that night.

The fear of death did not seem to have much of an impact on other teens. One of Ryan's friends, Paul Lynch, stated: "I don't think a lot of people are going to stop drinking because of Ryan's death. A lot of my friends drink to ease the pain of growing up. Problems at home, divorce." One student at Ryan's high school was quoted as saying: "If Goldie were here, he would want us to [continue drinking]. He'd tell us, 'Don't stop partying.'"

A few days after Ryan died, a group of students drove out to the crash site to toast "Goldie." They created a shrine to Ryan where students left empty beer cans in his memory. The principal of Verona High School also noted that several students showed up drunk at Ryan's funeral. She saw this as the "ultimate denial" of the problem.

Jim Goldsmith is committed to using Ryan's life as an example for other kids. He goes to high schools and speaks to students about the dangers of drinking and driving. "I can hold their attention for a moment. When I talk to kids, I make them cry. I make them feel the pain I felt losing a son. But what I don't know is how to make it stick with them. I wish I had that answer."

## Applying the LISTEN Process

Direct the students to their casebook, or photocopy and distribute the LISTEN process handout on page 209 for use with the students.

# PEACEMAKING
Handling Conflict with Creativity

### Discussion-Starter: Letters to the Editor

*Vary the way you discuss and process the cases in your classroom. Try this idea during one of the cases in this section.*

Before discussing the case in large group, ask the students to write an editorial regarding the case. Instruct the students to not sign their name. Then collect the anonymous letters. Fold the letters in half and put them in a box. Divide the class into groups and give each group one of the anonymous letters. If you have many classes of the same course, use the anonymous letters from different classes. Ask each group to collaborate on a response to the writer. Share the letters and responses with the large group and let the discussion move from there!

## Faith Application

After discussing the cases in this theme, ask the students to consider an action step that would move what they have learned out into the world. Consider these possibilities:

- learning more about the legal system and what measures are taken to keep from imprisoning innocent people
- finding out if there is a chapter of the Ulster Project International near you or how to start one in your community
- organizing an Amnesty International committee at your school
- encouraging the social studies department to include a unit on non-violence in the curriculum
- becoming involved with the Fellowship of Reconciliation and promoting peaceful conflict resolution within your school

## Opening Prayer

*(See handout on next page.)*

# A Prayer for Peacemaking

*Leader:* Peace flows from God. We can learn to be channels of that peace in our life. Let us listen to the words of Saint Paul to the Romans in Romans 12:14–18.

> Bless those who persecute you; bless and do not curse them. Rejoice with those who rejoice, weep with those who weep. Live in harmony with one another; do not be haughty, but associate with the lowly; do not claim to be wiser than you are. Do not repay anyone evil for evil, but take thought for what is noble in the sight of all. If it is possible, so far as it depends on you, live peaceably with all.

*All:* Shalom. God's peace dwell in us. Shalom.

*Reader 1:* When we are faced with conflict and pain, let us find a way to solve it peacefully.

*All:* Shalom. God's peace dwell in us. Shalom.

*Reader 2:* When hatred stares us in the face, let us find a way to meet it eye to eye with love.

*All:* Shalom. God's peace dwell in us. Shalom.

*Reader 3:* When doubts plague us and fear rises up within, let us embrace the questions and live with hope.

*All:* Shalom. God's peace dwell in us. Shalom.

*Reader 4:* When we are accused unfairly, let us be generous with forgiveness.

*All:* Shalom. God's peace dwell in us. Shalom. Amen.

# Resources for Peacemaking Case 1

## Case Focus: Forgiveness

Throughout the discussion of the case, bring up the following points and have the students apply and reflect upon them:
- We practice *peacemaking* when we try to resolve the inevitable conflicts of life in a creative, loving way.
- When Jesus said, "Love your enemies," he was not counseling passivity in the face of injustice but rather an active, constructive confrontation that does not return one harm with another harm.
- We are called to love our enemy as God loves each person and to forgive an unlimited number of times.

## *Catechism* Connections

Read the following passages in the *Catechism,* and ask the students to explain how the faith statements can be applied to this case:
- Living Jesus' commandment to love one another also means forgiving each other. (no. 2842)
- Forgiveness can be a transforming event that turns injury into compassion. (no. 2843)
- Forgiving our enemies is the way to reconciliation. (no. 2844)

## Scripture Connections

*The Catholic Youth Bible* includes articles on forgiveness:
- "Letting Go of the Past" (see Gen 33.1–17)
- "Letting Go of Anger" (see Psalm 103)
- "Forgive Us Our Debts" (see Mt 18.21–35)
- "The Reunion Dinner" (see Lk 7.1–10)

## Course Connections

This case can be used with the course *Growing in Christian Morality* in the chapter on peacemaking:
- turning the other cheek (p. 273)
- creative strategies for peacemaking (pp. 277–280)
- loving one's enemies (pp. 280–282)

## Research for Peacemaking Case 1: Wrongly Accused

Exact numbers are not available for how many people are in prison unjustly. Some researchers claim as many as 5 percent of those in prison are sent there based on eyewitness identification. If the number was just 1 percent, that would mean one thousand innocent people each year are wrongly imprisoned.

What is the reliability of eyewitness testimony? Gary Wells, PhD in psychology at Iowa State University, has studied human memory and says that it can fail us for two reasons.:

- "We're not programmed well to pick out a stranger from a lineup of similar people when we've seen that stranger on only one occasion." Cross-racial identifications are even more difficult.

- "An eyewitness identification is among the least reliable type of evidence, but it is among the most persuasive to a jury. How confident was the witness at the time of the photo spread? That's what's important, not her level of confidence at the trial. Memory doesn't get better with time."

## Follow-up for Peacemaking Case 1: Wrongly Accused

Jennifer Thompson is married and has triplets. She has become an outspoken opponent of the death penalty and speaks frequently about the unreliability of eyewitness testimony. She is a guest on talk shows and is thinking about writing a book. She says that Ronald Cotton has taught her a great deal about forgiveness, faith, and healing.

Ronald Cotton received a $110,000 settlement from the state of North Carolina for being unfairly incarcerated. He bought a house in the country with the money and married a co-worker from the insulation factory where he works. He and his wife have a baby girl.

# The LISTEN Process Applied

Use the sample questions below to help the students work through the application of the LISTEN process for this case. You may wish to suggest questions for the students or focus on one particular section of the process.

## Look for the Facts

1. What are the key facts in this situation?
2. Why was Ronald arrested and convicted on the rape charge?
3. Why was Ronald released from prison? How did this information come about?

## Imagine Possibilities

1. What basic choices did Ronald have for dealing with his unjust imprisonment?
2. How could creativity have been exercised in this situation?
3. What is the most loving response Ronald could have made?
4. What choices did Jennifer face when she learned that Ronald was innocent?

## Seek Insight Beyond Your Own

1. What advice would your parents and friends give you if you were blamed for something you did not do?
2. What legal issues were involved in this case? Whom would you turn to for legal advice?
3. Jesus was prosecuted unfairly and crucified for these unjust charges. How might his life provide some insights into this case?
4. If you were in Jennifer's situation, instrumental in putting someone in prison who did not belong there, whom would you turn to for advice?

## Turn Inward

1. How would your personal feelings come to play if you were in Ronald's situation? Jennifer's? How might past experiences come to play in each?
2. What motive did Jennifer have for wishing to meet with Ronald? How conflicted would you feel in this situation? Why?
3. If you were the unjustly accused, what would you want to come from a meeting with the one who put you in jail?
4. Would forgiveness be on your mind if you were Ronald? Why or why not?
5. If you were in Jennifer's situation, would you want to seek forgiveness from Ronald?

## Expect God's Help

1. Read Matthew 5:10–12. How might that Scripture reading comfort and challenge you if you were Ronald?
2. What prayer would you pray if you were in Jennifer's position after finding out that Ronald was innocent?

## Name Your Decision

1. Would you decide to reconcile with your accused?
2. What core values are being upheld in living out that decision?
3. What would you decide to do in Jennifer's situation?

### Final Questions and Thoughts on Peacemaking Case 1: Wrongly Accused

1. Whom do you most identify with in this case? Why?
2. How does this story illustrate the concept of reconciliation?
3. What thoughts do you have about the legal system after reading this case?
4. What lingering questions or thoughts do you have after reflecting on this case?

### Wrongly Accused

Ronald Cotton was one of eight children raised by a single mother in a poor neighborhood in North Carolina. He dropped out of school in the ninth grade, and his police record included convictions for breaking and entering and sexual assault. "I had it rough, coming up," Ronald has said. "I took the wrong route sometimes."

At age twenty-two, Ronald was working as a part-time cook at a seafood restaurant. On one hot, steamy night in July, two women living near the restaurant where he worked were raped in their homes.

Jennifer Thompson, a twenty-two-year-old college student, lived alone. That night she heard a noise and woke up to discover someone in her bedroom with a knife. "Hey, baby, how you doing? Shut up or I'll kill you," the voice said. Jennifer offered her money and credit cards, but the man wanted something else. He proceeded to brutally rape her. Knowing that she was not capable of fighting him because he was so much bigger than her, Jennifer tried to memorize details about him—his face, eyes, hair, and voice.

After he raped her, Jennifer told him she needed to go to the bathroom, and he let her. She turned on the light and got a better view of the rapist. She also told him she needed a drink of water. When she went to the kitchen, she threw ice in the sink loudly, noticed the back door was ajar, covered herself with a blanket, and ran to a nearby home. Jennifer was taken to the hospital for a rape examination kit. While there she learned that another woman had been raped less than a mile from her home only an hour and a half later. This strengthened her desire to convict the attacker.

Two days after working with the police department to create a sketch of the rapist, Jennifer was called in to look at six photographs. All these men had criminal records and had photos filed with the police. Jennifer clearly identified Ronald Cotton's picture.

Later that day, Ronald went home and was told that the police were looking for him. He immediately drove to the police station to clear things up. He was not nervous because he knew he had not committed the crime. But once he got to the police department, Ronald found that the police had discovered that his shoes matched the ones Jennifer described. A flashlight that was identical to the one stolen from the other victim was found at his home. Ronald's alibi that he was with friends did not check out because his friends denied it. This circumstantial evidence, along with his police record and Jennifer's choosing him from a photo lineup, was enough to get Ronald arrested. During the physical lineup, Ronald had to speak the words Jennifer remembered her attacker saying: "Hey, baby, how you doing? Shut up or I'll kill you." Jennifer identified him as the man who raped her.

Months later Ronald Cotton was convicted of first-degree burglary and first-degree rape. He was sentenced to life plus fifty years in prison. Jennifer Thompson claimed that this day was the happiest day of her life, and she toasted the conviction of Ronald Cotton with champagne.

Ronald began serving his time and told himself over and over, "The Lord don't put nothing on you you can't bear." Ronald filed an appeal and wrote many letters to his attorney. He said, "I developed a big callus on my finger from all the letter writing."

In prison, Ronald overheard Bobby Poole, an inmate from the same town who was also convicted of rape, claim that Ronald was serving time for a crime that Bobby had actually committed. Ronald wrote his lawyer again with this information, and a couple years later another trial was granted. There Jennifer saw Ronald side-by-side with Bobby. Jennifer's testimony did not change, and Ronald was convicted again.

Ronald was back in prison with Bobby Poole. "It was hard. I wanted to really hurt this guy. But my father, he told me—he said, 'No, don't do it. Just let his conscience eat him, and eventually, you know, he'll confess.'"

Years went by and Ronald remained incarcerated. During those years DNA testing became part of forensic science and became key evidence in the courts. When Ronald learned of this technology, he became convinced that it would prove his innocence. He contacted Rich Rosen, a law professor at the University of North Carolina, who agreed to work on Ronald's case. Evidence from the rape kits still existed, and scientists were able to isolate a tiny fragment of sperm that could be used in a test against Ronald's DNA. It was not a match. When the lab tested the sample against Bobby Poole's DNA, they found that he was the rapist. When confronted with the evidence, Bobby did not deny it. Eleven years after his original conviction, Ronald Cotton was released from prison, pardoned, and was a free man.

When Jennifer was told about this, she fell apart. "The guilt got so heavy and the nightmares were still there," she remembered. "I was literally dying with the guilt."

Jennifer decided that she needed to meet Ronald face to face. The police captain set it up, and Ronald agreed to it, saying: "There [were] a lot of unanswered questions lingering in my head. I just wanted to hear what she had to say."

Two years later Ronald and Jennifer met in a church in the same town where the rape occurred. Jennifer thanked Ronald for meeting her. Then she said: "I could spend every day for the rest of my life telling you how sorry I am and it wouldn't be enough. Can you ever forgive me?"

She started to cry. Ronald replied: "I don't hate you. I've never hated you. I forgive you, and I want you to have a good life. And I want to have a good life."

The meeting transformed their lives. Jennifer said: "Ronald Cotton has allowed me to ask for forgiveness. That is a gift. . . . I feel very grateful to him. I think he's an amazing human being."

## Applying the LISTEN Process

Direct the students to their casebook, or photocopy and distribute the LISTEN process handout on page 209 for use with the students.

# Resources for Peacemaking Case 2

## Case Focus: Images of the Enemy as Brothers and Sisters

Throughout the discussion of the case, bring up the following points and have the students apply and reflect on them:

- We practice *peacemaking* when we try to resolve the inevitable conflicts of life in a creative, loving way.
- When Jesus said, "Love your enemies," he was not counseling passivity in the face of injustice, but rather he was confronting injustice in an active way that does not return harm with harm.
- Peacemaking in interpersonal conflict calls for creative strategies: acknowledging our feelings, stating what is bothering us without attacking, being sincere in listening to the other person, and not retaliating.

## *Catechism* Connections

Read the following passages in the *Catechism,* and ask the students to explain how the faith statements can be applied to this case:

- Forgiveness can be a transforming event that turns injury into compassion. (no. 2843)
- Forgiving our enemies is the way to reconciliation. (no. 2844)

## Scripture Connections

*The Catholic Youth Bible* includes articles that build on the themes in this case:

- "Becoming a Peacemaker" (see Rom 12.17–19)
- "A Real Love" (see Rom 13.8–10)
- "Respecting Differences" (see Rom 14.1–23)

## Course Connections

This case can be used with the course *Growing in Christian Morality* with the chapter on peacemaking:

- turning the other cheek (p. 273)
- creative strategies for peacemaking (pp. 277–280)
- loving one's enemies (pp. 280–282)
- world peacemaking (pp. 283–284)

## Literature Connection

The novel *Joshua and the Children* by Joseph F. Girzone (New York: Simon and Schuster, 1989) is a parable that places Joshua (Jesus) in a country divided by violence and corruption. The story parallels the situation in Northern Ireland. This is an excellent novel to use with students.

## Research for Peacemaking Case 2: Waging Peace

You can pursue further research on this topic by searching Web sites for Northern Ireland and the Ulster Project International or by logging on to our Faith Community Builders Web site, *www.smp.org/bs,* and searching the links and resources provided there.

# The LISTEN Process Applied

Use the sample questions below to help the students work through the application of the LISTEN process for this case. You may wish to suggest questions for the students or focus on one particular section of the process.

## Look for the Facts

1. What basic decision did the Irish teens have to make?
2. Why is the hatred so strong between Catholics and Protestants in Northern Ireland?

## Imagine Possibilities

1. What are all the ways that Cheryl, Rachel, and Catherine could deal with the violence and hatred in their country?
2. What potential outcomes could come from each of these options? (You may wish to use the consequence tree handout on page 208 for this activity.)
3. How is the Ulster Project International a creative way to deal with the issue of hatred? How is it a systemic approach to the problems?
4. How is being involved with the Ulster Project International potentially dangerous for the teenagers?

## Seek Insight Beyond Your Own

1. If you were surrounded by hatred against another group of people in your town, to whom would you turn for advice? Why?
2. Consider the story of the good Samaritan. What would Jesus advise the teens to do in this situation?

## Turn Inward

1. How would you feel if you were persecuted for your religion or if you were in the minority? Why?
2. What role would your life experiences and family background play in making a decision to befriend an "enemy?"
3. At your gut level, would you be drawn to segregation or collaboration with someone from a different religion or someone identified as an "enemy"?

## Expect God's Help

1. Compose a prayer for peace and unity in Northern Ireland.
2. Read Matthew 5:43–45. How might that Scripture reading comfort and challenge you if you were a teen in Northern Ireland?

## Name Your Decision

1. How would you choose to deal with the intense hatred and division in your homeland if you were a teen in Northern Ireland?
2. Would you choose to get involved with the Ulster Project International?
3. What core values are being upheld in living out that decision?

### Final Questions and Thoughts on Peacemaking Case 2: Waging Peace

1. Whom do you most identify with in this case? Why?
2. What is at the root of hatred and persecution?
3. Is hatred taught? How?
4. What lingering questions or thoughts do you have after reflecting on this case?

# Peacemaking Case 2

## Waging Peace

Northern Ireland is a country with deep divisions and a history of violence. Catholics have long been a minority in the country, facing many disadvantages. A civil rights movement that gained momentum in the late 1960s brought British troops to take up permanent residence in Northern Ireland, also known as Ulster. In 1972 these British soldiers shot and killed thirteen protestors during a civil rights march. This came to be known as "Bloody Sunday." The hatred runs deep between Catholics and Protestants and is passed on to new generations.

The Ulster Project International is a program designed to break down and heal the divisions between Catholic and Protestant teenagers from Northern Ireland. They come to the United States and are paired with American teens of the same age, sex, and religion. A month of activities planned for the Irish and American teens brings them together to get to know each other outside their divided country.

Catherine and Rachel, one a Catholic and one a Protestant, grew up in a town in Northern Ireland where religion determines everything, including the soccer team that a person cheers for. Catholics cheer for the Celtics and Protestants cheer for the Rangers. While in the United States, some Catholics wore Rangers jerseys and Protestants wore shirts for the Celtics. Another girl, a Protestant, had something to say about the shirt swapping: "Frankly, if you did that at home, you would get beat up."

While participating in the Ulster Project, Catherine and Rachel visited an amusement park and rode a roller coaster together. Both wished their time together could have lasted longer. Cheryl, another Irish teen, commented that she could never go to an amusement park with a Catholic at home because segregation by religion is part of life in her hometown.

While these teens participated in the Ulster Project, their last names could not be identified for safety reasons. Any political statements could be used against them or their families back home, according to Marie House, the Chattanooga, Tennessee, chapter director of the Ulster Project.

During their visit to the United States, the Irish teens learned that a car bomb exploded in their hometown. That was a painful reminder that the violence continues even as they begin to learn how to collaborate and build peace between each other. "These kids haven't worked together before they came here," House said. "We are laying the groundwork that makes them realize they are equal."

## Applying the LISTEN Process

Direct the students to their casebook, or photocopy and distribute the LISTEN process handout on page 209 for use with the students.

## Following Her Conscience

### Case Focus: Participating in War, Conscientious Objection

Throughout the discussion of the case, bring up the following points and have the students apply and reflect on them:
- When Jesus said, "Love your enemies," he was not counseling passivity in the face of injustice, but rather he was confronting injustice in an active way that does not return harm with harm.
- Peacemaking in interpersonal conflict calls for creative strategies: acknowledging our feelings, stating what is bothering us without attacking, being sincere in listening to the other person, and not retaliating.
- We practice peacemaking when we reflect on our own participation in war. The Catholic hierarchy supports conscientious objector status as an option, which involves making a decision not to participate in war based on the conviction that war is immoral.
- In choosing a job or career, we need to question whether our choice fosters justice and peace.

### *Catechism* Connections

Read the following passages in the *Catechism,* and ask the students to explain how the faith statements can be applied to this case:
- We are obliged to work together to avoid war. (no. 2308)
- Those who serve their country in the military are called to do so honorably. (no. 2310)
- Provisions should be made for conscientious objectors. (no. 2311)

### Scripture Connections

*The Catholic Youth Bible* includes articles on war that pertain to this case:
- "Facing Life's Battles" (see Deut 20.1)
- "Wartime Women" (see Judges, chapter 4)
- "The Battle Within" (see Judges, chapter 4)
- "A Just War" (see 1 Macc 6)
- "Nonviolent Resistance" (see 2 Macc 8)

## Course Connections

This case can be used with the course *Growing in Christian Morality* with the chapter on peacemaking:

- creative strategies for peacemaking (pp. 277–280)
- participating in war, conscientious objection (pp. 285–286)
- loving one's enemies (pp. 280–282)

## Research for Peacemaking Case 3: Following Her Conscience

You can pursue further research on this topic by searching Web sites for the National Interreligious Service Board for Conscientious Objectors, the Fellowship of Reconciliation, or by logging on to our Faith Community Builders Web site, *www.smp.org/hs,* and searching the links and resources provided there.

## Follow-Up for Peacemaking Case 3: Following Her Conscience

- The military recognizes that people can change their mind about participation in the service. This is referred to as *crystallization.* Crystallization can occur when someone in the service realizes what it means to take a human life and recognizes that he or she cannot do that.
- The U.S. military requires that crystallization and the objection to war apply to *all* wars. International organizations, including the United Nations and Amnesty International, allow for conscientious objection to a particular war.
- During the Gulf War, 229 people applied for conscientious objector status. After review 140 of these applications were granted.

# The LISTEN Process Applied

Use the sample questions below to help the students work through the application of the LISTEN process for this case. You may wish to suggest questions for the students or focus on one particular section of the process.

## Look for the Facts

1. What is the critical decision that Yolanda faced?
2. What facts would you want to know before making a decision to become a conscientious objector or to report to war duty?
3. What were the circumstances surrounding the Persian Gulf War and Operation Desert Storm?

## Imagine Possibilities

1. What options did Yolanda have for dealing with her belief that the war in the Persian Gulf was not one that she wished to participate in?
2. What short- and long-term consequences would be part of each option? (You may wish to use the consequence tree handout on page 208 for this activity.)

## Seek Insight Beyond Your Own

1. What advice would your parents give you in this situation?
2. What advice would you expect from your friends?
3. What legal issues are involved in obtaining conscientious objector status or deserting the Army?
4. How could the underlying values found in the fifth commandment, "You shall not kill," provide guidance in this situation?
5. What does the church teach about conscientious objector status and involvement in war?

## Turn Inward

1. What would motivate you to choose to desert or file for conscientious objector status?
2. What does your conscience say to you about this situation?
3. What life experiences could come to play in making this decision?
4. What could possibly cause a change of heart like the one Yolanda, someone who had been in the Army for five years before this situation, experienced?

## Expect God's Help

1. What prayer would you offer for someone struggling with the decision whether to go to war?
2. Read Psalm 3. How might that Scripture reading comfort and challenge you if you were in Yolanda's position?

## Name Your Decision

1. What decision would you have made if you were Yolanda? Why?
2. What core values are being upheld in living out that decision?

### Final Questions and Thoughts on Peacemaking Case 3: Following Her Conscience

1. Whom do you most identify with in this case? Why?
2. Do you think that someone in the military could change his or her mind about the service during wartime? Why?
3. Should there be long-term consequences for those who desert or go AWOL from military service? What types of consequences?
4. What lingering questions or thoughts do you have after reflecting on this case?

## Following Her Conscience

Yolanda Huet-Vaughn grew up in Mexico, where as a young Catholic girl, one of her heroes was Saint Joan of Arc, a martyred soldier of faith. Yolanda became an American citizen and later joined the Army Reserves in college because of her love of adventure and because it was a way to pay her tuition bills. Her family also had a strong patriotic background.

Yolanda became a doctor and served in the Army Reserves. "All I did for six years was give physicals," she said. She left with an honorable discharge in 1982.

Seven years later, Yolanda was married, a mother of three, and was working as a family doctor at Humana Health Care in Kansas City. When the Berlin Wall came down, Yolanda remembered that she still owed the Army two years of service even though she had been discharged. She re-enlisted because she "wanted to be part of the 'New World Order'" and she felt morally obligated.

When the war broke out in the Persian Gulf, Yolanda was called to active duty with her unit. She was assigned to work in an army hospital in Saudi Arabia. When the unit shipped out in December 1990, Yolanda did not report. "I just walked out the door," she said.

"I felt that we were basically going to a war by a deadline that was avoidable, that would, in fact, if we proceeded with it, create over one hundred thousand civilian casualties; would potentially put at risk fifty thousand American lives; and I said, 'No. This is an avoidable catastrophe. It is something we need to stand up [to] and say we will not act in this war. We have alternatives.'"

The military did not agree, and Yolanda was held under house arrest for four months, then court-martialed and imprisoned in Fort Leavenworth for eight months of a thirty-month sentence.

Yolanda recognized the consequences of her actions and that her husband and children could suffer because of her beliefs. "But this goes against my principles as a physician and a human being. We're talking about leading people to slaughter."

Yolanda continued to be outspoken in her dissent. "I was punished as harshly as possible because I made myself as visible as possible. The Army could not silence or control me. I love America and expect our leaders to act honorably. I had to speak out against a war fought not for democracy, but to keep on the throne a Kuwaiti king with seventy-five wives. I was right to do this and I wish I was even more successful in getting my message across. I regret that I couldn't help stop the deaths from hunger and the poor situation of fifty thousand Iraqi children in 1992—collateral casualties of our war on them."

When Yolanda was put in jail, a scandal followed. Amnesty International named her as a "prisoner of conscience." A former attorney general spoke out in her defense. She was also given a prestigious award by the Physicians Forum that recognized her "political integrity and personal courage in defending the public health by refusing active duty."

On 7 April 1992, Yolanda was released. The Kansas Board of Healing Arts tried to revoke her medical license because she committed a felony by deserting the Army. She lost her good job at Human Health Care and considered moving away from Kansas. She later said: "This is our home and our community. My roots are here and there is still a great deal that needs to be done. Maybe someday we will all transcend political differences and just support one another."

## Applying the LISTEN Process

Direct the students to their casebook, or photocopy and distribute the LISTEN process handout on page 209 for use with the students.

# Consequence Tree

Every *decision* involves a number of *options,* and each of these options has a number of possible *consequences.* Use this handout to help you visualize your options and their consequences.

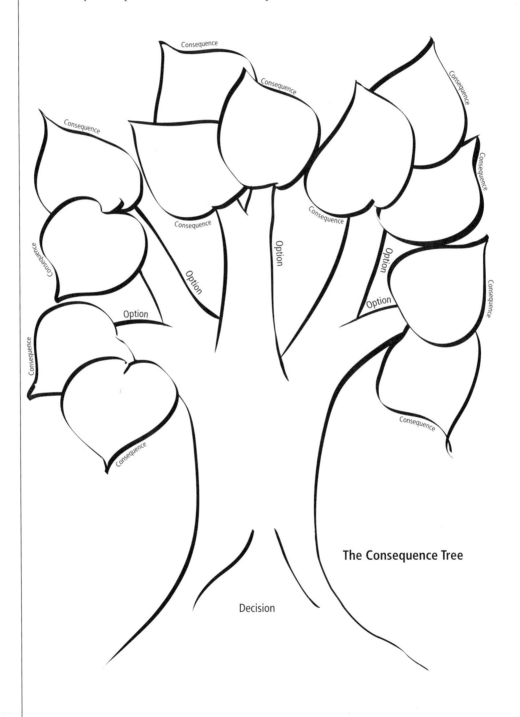

**The Consequence Tree**

# The LISTEN Process

Use the LISTENing steps and space below to reflect on the cases you have read.

Case _____

**L**ook for the Facts

**I**magine Possibilities

**S**eek Insight Beyond Your Own

**T**urn Inward

**E**xpect God's Help

**N**ame Your Decision

**Handout L**

## Acknowledgments *(continued from page 4)*

The scriptural quotation on page 101 is from the New Amercian Bible. Copyright © 1991, 1986, and 1970 by the Confraternity of Christian Doctrine, Washington, DC 20017-1194. All rights reserved.

All other scriptural quotations are from the New Revised Standard Version of the Bible. Copyright © 1989 by the Division of Christian Education of the National Council of the Churches of Christ in the United States of America. All rights reserved.

All references to the *Catechism* are references to the *Catechism of the Catholic Church* for the United States of America. Copyright © 1994 by the United States Conference of Catholic Bishops (USCCB)—Libreria Editrice Vaticana. English translation of the *Catechism of the Catholic Church: Modifications from the Editio Typica* copyright © 1997 by the USCCB—Libreria Editrice Vaticana.

Judgment Case 1: A Deadly Practical Joke is adapted from David Barham's "Innocent Prank Turns into Tragedy," Gannet News Service (8 November 1994).

The quotations in Follow-up for Judgment Case 2: Stop-Sign Prank and in Judgment Case 2: Stop-Sign Prank are from "Foolish and Deadly," an interview hosted by Elizabeth Vargas on *ABC's 20/20* (17 October 1997).

The quotation on page 23 is from "School Pranks Hardly Innocent: Teens' Antics Increasingly Destructive," *Dallas Morning News* (9 June 2000).

Justice Case 1: Blowing the Whistle is adapted from Richard Jerome and Vickie Bane's "A Montana Woman Blows the Whistle on the Asbestos Mine That Killed Her Parents and Ravaged Her Town," *People* (2 October 2000).

The sexual harassment statistics on page 37 are taken from John Phillips's "Sexual Harassment Seen As Reality for U.S. Teens," Reuter's (6 September 1996).

Justice Case 2: Harassment at School is adapted from Melba Newsome's "Sexually Harassed at School," *Twist* (September 1999).

Justice Case 3: Appropriate Punishment, or Torture? is adapted from David Grogan, Karen Emmons, Luchina Fisher, and Tom Nugent's "Whipping Boy: U.S. Teenager Michael Fay Pleads with Singapore to Spare the Rod," *People* (18 April 1994).

The quotation by Irene Opdyke on page 54 is from Elisa Willis's "Irene's Choice Saved Twelve: A Friendship Endures Horror of Holocaust," *Newsday* (29 March 1993).

Courage Case 1: Rescuing Friendship is adapted from Daphne Eviatar's "Hands of Heroism: A Holocaust Rescuer Who Held Hope and Life for Persecuted Jews," *Newsday* (18 August 1999); "A Whisper from Above," an interview hosted by Cynthia McFadden and Sam Donaldson on *ABC Primetime Live* (10 June 1998); Michael Precker's "Secret Pacts, Saved Lives: Irene Gut Opdyke, a Polish Catholic, Hid Jews from Nazis and Didn't Count the Cost," *Dallas Morning News* (29 November 1999); and Elisa Willis's "Irene's Choice Saved Twelve: A Friendship Endures Horror of Holocaust," *Newsday* (29 March 1993).

The quotation on page 59 is from Bill Hewitt and Khoi Nguyen's "On the Wings of an Eagle: When Boy Scout Henry Nicols Got AIDS, He Was Prepared for Anything—Except Surrender," *People* (10 June 1991).

Courage Case 2: Staring Down AIDS is adapted from Dinah Eng's "Mountains to Climb," Gannet News Service (3 July 1995); and Bill Hewitt and Khoi Nguyen's "On the Wings of an Eagle: When Boy Scout Henry Nicols Got AIDS, He Was Prepared for Anything—Except Surrender," *People* (10 June 1991).

Courage Case 3: Saving Her Children is adapted from Chris Poytner's "Mother, Children Mourned at Funeral," *Courier-Journal* (7 June 2000); and Shannon Tangonan's "Mother Who Tried to Save Children from Blaze Dies," *Courier-Journal* (3 June 2000).

Wholeness Case 1: Living High is adapted from Renee Kohl's "Semi-Charmed Life," *Seventeen* (September 2000).

Wholeness Case 2: Teen Parents is adapted from Jeanne Marie Laskas's "Someone to Love," *Good Housekeeping* 223 (1 August 1996).

Wholeness Case 3: Dying to Be Whole is adapted from Bill Hewitt, Gabrielle Saveri, Ken Baker, Lyndon Stambler, and Julie Jordan's "Last Dance: A Desperate Desire to Be Slender May Have Cost Twenty-two-year-old Ballerina Heidi Guenther Her Life," *People* (28 July 1997).

The quotation on page 88 is from Anastasia Toufexis's "Shortcut to the Rambo Look: Ninety-seven-pound Weaklings No More, Teens Take Steroids to Bulk Up," *Time* (30 January 1989).

Wholeness Case 4: Bulking Up is adapted from Natalie Angier's "Is G.I. Joe Leading His Troops in the Right Direction? Some Worry That Young Athletes Will Go to Extremes to Copy Him," *Minneapolis Star Tribune* (1 February 1999); Anastasia Toufexis's "Shortcut to the Rambo Look: Ninety-seven-pound Weaklings No More, Teens Take Steroids to Bulk Up," *Time* (30 January 1989); and Jerome M. Schrof's "Pumped Up," *U.S. News and World Report* (1 June 1992).

Honesty Case 1: Driving Honesty is adapted from Margot Dougherty's "Happy: Driving Along Minding His Business, Melvin Kiser Ran into Two Million Dollars—Then He Did the Unthinkable," *People* (30 November 1987).

Honesty Case 2: An Epidemic of Cheating is adapted from Noelle Howey's "Look Who's Cheating," *Teen People* (October 2000).

The statistics on page 103 are taken from "Troubling Sign for the Future," *Atlanta Journal* (17 October 2000).

Honesty Case 3: Little Big Lies is adapted from Susan Jacoby's "The Truth About Lies: Little Ones Can Have Big Consequences," *Cosmopolitan* 218 (1 January 1995).

People Case 1: Abusive Relationships is adapted from a transcript called "Dating Violence: Twisted Love," accessed at *www.pbs.org/inthemix/shows/transcript_dating_violence.html* (1 February 2001).

People Case 2: Who Belongs? is adapted from Rebecca McCarthy's "Sorority Racial Snub a 'Wake-up Call,'" accessed at *www.accessatlanta.com/partners/ajc/newsatlanta/uga_sorority.html* (16 September 2000); and a letter from an anonymous woman to Dr. Richard M. Ross, Assistant Vice President for Student Affairs at the University of Georgia, accessed at *www.accessatlanta.com/partners/ajc/newsatlanta/uga_letter.html* (16 September 2000).

People Case 3: Intimidation and Compassion Case 1: Getting to Know Angie are adapted from Andrea Heiman's "Hurt by Hate," *Teen* (October 1994).

Compassion Case 2: A Change of Heart is adapted from "The Verdict in the Oklahoma City Bombing Trial," an interview hosted by Chris Wallace on *ABC News Nightline* (2 June 1997); Doug Carroll's "From Oklahoma City to Home, We Must Forgive to Move On," *Arizona Republic* (14 March 2000); Lois Romano's "Mixed Feelings in a Murder Case: Oklahoma Torn Over New Trial for Nichols," *Washington Post* (6 May 2000); and "Oklahoma City: Four Years Later," an interview hosted by Bob McNamara on *CBS Evening News with Dan Rather* (19 April 1999).

Creation Case 1: Caring for the Environment is adapted from Maile Carpenter's "Preserving Paradise," *Teen People* (August 2000).

Creation Case 2: Simple Living is adapted from "Simplicity Enriches Life for 'Basics' Families: More People Are Choosing a Life That Allows Them to Live Within Their Values," *Minneapolis Star Tribune* (14 February 1999).

Creation Case 3: Trees Can Help is adapted from "Planting Trees of Life: I Don't Like the Title Dreamer. . . . That Tends to Mean Nondeliverer," *Time* (9 January 1989); Michelle Derrow's "The Forest: Helping Earth, Tree by Tree," *Time for Kids* (2 October 1998); and Tracy Rysavy's "Tree People," accessed at *www.futurenet.org/12Climatechange/rysavy. html* (22 November 2000).

The quote on page 163 by George Annas is taken from Anastasia Toufexis's "Creating a Child to Save Another: A 'Miracle Baby' Promises Both Blessings and Controversy," *Time* (5 March 1990).

The quotes on page 163 by Dr. Steven Foreman and Alexander Capron are taken from "Born to Give," an interview hosted by Bob Brown, Hugh Downs, and Barbara Walters on *ABC's 20/20* (6 November 1997).

The four guiding principals for considering moral issues that involve medical technology on page 164 is adapted from *Instruction on Respect for Human Life in its Origin and the Dignity of Procreation: Replies to Certain Questions of the Day,* by the Congregation for the Doctrine of Faith, accessed at *listserv.american.edu/catholic/church/vatican/giftlife.doc* (2 February 2001).

Reverence Case 1: Sisters for Life is adapted from Anastasia Toufexis's "Creating a Child to Save Another: A 'Miracle Baby' Promises Both Blessings and Controversy," *Time* (5 March 1990); "Born to Give," an interview hosted by Bob Brown, Hugh Downs, and Barbara Walters on *ABC's 20/20* (6 November 1997); and David Grogan, Nancy Matsumoto, and Kristina Johnson's "To Save Their Daughter From Leukemia, Abe and Mary Ayala Conceived a Plan—And a Baby," *People* (5 March 1990).

Reverence Case 2: Mother and Daughter is adapted from "Birthday: Now They Are One," *People* (26 October 1992); J. Madeleine and Nash Aberdeen's "All in the Family: How Does That Gutsy South Dakota Grandma Feel About Being Pregnant with Her Daughter's Twins?" *Time* (19 August 1991); William Plummer and Margaret Nelson's "A Mother's Priceless Gift: Unable to Bear Children, An Iowa Woman Found a Surrogate She Could Trust—Her Mom," *People* (26 August 1991); and Sasha Nyary's "The Way We Live: Miraculous Babies," *Life* (1 December 1993).

Reverence Case 3: A Time to Die is adapted from Theresa Tighe's "Christine Busalacchi Dies at Twenty-two: Father Says 'Nobody Won,' As Life, Legal Struggle End," *St. Louis Post-Dispatch* (8 March 1993); "'Key Events' in Busalacchi Case," *St. Louis Post-Dispatch* (8 March 1993); "The Long Death of Christine Busalacchi," *St. Louis Post-Dispatch* (9 March 1993); and Joe Holleman's "Barnes' Diagnosis Is Same: Busalacchi's Condition Vegetative, Doctors Say," *St. Louis Post-Dispatch* (25 February 1993).

The quotations on page 191 are taken from Dennis Covington's "What Jennifer Can Never Forget," *Redbook* 190 (1 November 1997).

Peacemaking Case 1: Wrongly Accused is adapted from Dennis Covington's "What Jennifer Can Never Forget," *Redbook* 190 (1 November 1997); "The Man of Her Nightmares," an interview hosted by Elizabeth Vargas and Barbara Walters on *ABC's 20/20* (27 July 1998); Claudia Glenn Dowling's "Mistaken Identity: Jennifer Thompson Knew That Ronald Cotton Was the Man Who Raped Her. She Was Wrong. Now, They Hope to Keep Others from Making the Same Tragic Error," *People* (14 August 2000); Cynthia Sanz and Sarah Skolnik's "Happy: Ticket to Walk After Eleven Years, DNA Spells Freedom for Ronald Cotton, Sent to Prison for Two Rapes He Did Not Commit," *People* (31 July 1995).

The quotations in Peacemaking Case 2: Waging Peace are taken from Jim Hannah's "Travel Project Brings Ulster's Catholics and Protestants Together in USA," Gannet News Service (31 July 1996).

Peacemaking Case 3: Following Her Conscience is adapted from Marlene C. Piturro's "Study War No More: The Price of Conscience," *On the Issues* 3 (1 June 1994); Michael Ryan and J. D. Podolsky's "The Call to Arms Has Sounded, But for Love of Peace, or Fear of War, Some Soldiers Are Just Saying No," *People* (4 February 1991); and "Gulf War 'Deserter' Fights to Retain Medical License," an interview reported by Nick Haynes, KANU, on National Public Radio's *All Things Considered* (17 October 1993).

## Art and Photo Credits

Shanna Bayer: pages 90, 92, 94, 96, 98, 100, 102, 104
Joseph Paul Church: cover (third from top), pages 105, 106, 108, 110, 112, 114, 116, 118, 120
Renee DeLellis: cover (first from top)
Betsy Holmes: pages 66, 68, 70, 72, 74, 76, 78, 80, 82, 84, 86, 88
Katie Jäger: pages 140, 142, 144, 146, 148, 150, 152, 154, 156
Samantha K. Keller: pages 27, 28, 30, 32, 34, 36, 38, 40, 42, 44, 46
Adrienne Maple: pages 122, 124, 126, 128, 130, 132, 134, 136, 138
Hannah Olson: pages 187, 188, 190, 192, 194, 196, 198, 200, 202, 204, 206
Lisa Schwichtenberg: cover (fourth from top)
Brian Sellers: pages 48, 50, 52, 54, 56, 58, 60, 62, 64
Noelle Tracey: pages 158, 160, 162, 164, 166, 168, 170, 172, 174, 176, 178, 180, 182, 184, 186
Sarah Wallace: pages 10, 12, 14, 16, 18, 20, 22, 24, 26

Laurie Geisler: page 208
SuperStock: cover (background), cover (second from top), pages 208, 210, 212